SAVE LIKE A HONEY BEE

*"Harnessing Nature's Wisdom
for Financial Abundance"*

Shamsud Zaman

COPYRIGHT

Disclaimer:

The information provided in this book, "Save Like a Honey Bee: Harnessing Nature's Wisdom for Financial Abundance," is for general informational purposes only. The author and publisher make no representation or warranties of any kind, express or implied, about the completeness, accuracy, reliability, suitability, or availability concerning the content, information, products, services, or related graphics contained in this book for any purpose. The author and publisher disclaim any liability for any loss or damage, including without limitation, indirect or consequential loss or damage, or any loss or damage whatsoever arising from loss of data or profits arising out of or in connection with the use of this book. Readers are advised to consult with financial professionals or other experts in their specific circumstances before making any financial decisions or implementing any strategies discussed in this book. The author and publisher shall not be responsible for any adverse consequences resulting from readers' decisions or actions based on the information provided in this publication. Every effort has been made to accurately represent the information in this book at the time of publication. However, the nature of financial information and practices may change over time, and the author and publisher are not obligated to update the content to reflect such changes. Any references to third-party websites, products, or services are for informational purposes only and do not constitute an endorsement or recommendation by the author or publisher. The author and publisher are not responsible for the content or practices of third-party entities. By reading this book, the reader acknowledges and agrees to the terms of this disclaimer and the limitations of the information provided herein.

PREFACE

Y ou are about to read "Save Like a Honey Bee: Harnessing Nature's Wisdom for Financial Abundance." This book is inspired by the honey bee, a remarkable creature that exhibits qualities of industriousness, collaboration, and strategic planning in the natural world. In this book, we will explore how the wisdom of the honey bee can help us achieve financial prudence and well-being.

Personal finance is an art that involves balancing earning, saving, and investing wisely. The honey bee colony provides a fascinating parallel for this art, as it operates with intricate systems of resource management, future planning, and collective decision-making. This book aims to provide insights, strategies, and a fresh perspective on how we can apply the principles of the honey bee to our financial lives.

The Essence of the Hive:

The honey bee is more than a nectar collector; it is a resource manager, a future planner, and a team player. As we examine the hive's collective wisdom, we will discover valuable lessons that align with prudent financial management. Each chapter will reveal a unique aspect of the honey bee's approach that we can adopt in our financial lives, such as precision in purpose, strategic saving, and risk diversification.

Beyond Metaphor: Practical Applications:

This book is not just a metaphorical exploration; it is also a practical guide. Each chapter will include real-world examples, data-driven analysis, and actionable strategies that you can implement in your financial journey. Whether you are an experienced investor, a diligent saver, or a beginner in personal finance, this book has something for you.

Acknowledging Nature's Teachers:

As we read "Save Like a Honey Bee," let us appreciate the small but powerful teachers from the natural world. The honey bees show us how to build financial abundance and resilience with their rhythmic dances, meticulous resource allocation, and collaborative endeavors.

A Journey Together:

This book is not a lecture; it is a conversation. I invite you to join me on this journey of learning from the hive mind, the disciplined dance of the honey bee, and the wisdom of nature. Together, we will gain a new perspective on how we approach wealth and prosperity.

Thank you for choosing this book. I hope it will inspire you to save like a honey bee and achieve financial abundance and a thriving future.

Sincerely,

Shamsud Ahmed,
31st Dec Pune/INDIA

PROLOGUE:

Nature is a rich source of wisdom, and among its many wonders, the honey bee stands out as a remarkable example of financial intelligence. In "Save Like a Honey Bee: Harnessing Nature's Wisdom for Financial Abundance," we embark on a journey that goes beyond the conventional wisdom of personal finance and taps into the timeless principles of nature.

As we begin this exploration, imagine a thriving hive, a harmonious community where each bee plays a vital role in the collective prosperity. This book is an invitation to learn, reflect, and apply the principles that enable the honey bee to achieve financial abundance and resilience in our own lives.

The Hive as a Blueprint:

The honey bee hive is not just a group of individuals; it is a living system of collaboration, efficient resource management, and adaptation to changing conditions. In the following pages, we will draw inspiration from the hive's complex structure, from the informative waggle dance to the optimal allocation of resources, and discover how these lessons can enhance our financial endeavors.

According to the USDA, the number of beehives in the US decreased from 6 to 2.5 million between 1940 and 2021, yet honey bees still pollinate more than 80% of the food crops in the US1. How do they manage to do that? What can we learn from their remarkable efficiency and productivity?

Lessons from the Dance of Bees:

The prologue sets the stage for a journey that takes us from the metaphorical to the practical. Each chapter is a focused exploration of a specific aspect of the honey bee's financial philosophy, offering insights that range from precision in purpose to the power of strategic saving.

According to NASA, an average beehive can hold around 50,000 bees, and each forager must collect nectar from about 2 million flowers to make 1 pound of honey2. The average forager makes only about 1/12th of a teaspoon of honey in her lifetime2. How do they achieve such a remarkable feat of collective saving? What can we learn from their disciplined and collaborative approach to building wealth?

A Call to Collaboration:

This is not a book to be read passively; it is a call to collaboration. Imagine this journey as a shared endeavor, with the honey bee as our guide. Together, we will navigate the financial landscapes, learn from the hive's disciplined dance, and emerge with a renewed perspective on how we can build wealth, cultivate resilience, and thrive in the face of financial challenges.

According to Pawsome Advice, a bee colony can lose 15%–20% of its population in one bad year3. Yet, honey bees are able to recover and sustain their colonies through changing seasons and environments. How do they cope with such losses and uncertainties? What can we learn from their adaptive and resilient strategies to overcome financial difficulties?

The Invitation:

As we turn the pages of "Save Like a Honey Bee," let us open our minds to the timeless lessons nature has to offer. The hive awaits, and within its buzzing chambers lies a wealth of wisdom waiting to be explored. May this journey be transformative, enlightening, and, above all, a step towards financial abundance.

Welcome to the hive.

CHAPTER 1

The Honey Bee's Financial Ballet

Within the heart of the hive, where the symphony of industrious wings intertwines with the dance of sunlight filtering through the entrance, an extraordinary spectacle unfolds—the honey bee's financial ballet. In this bustling microcosm, each bee assumes a pivotal role, and resources are allocated with a precision that rivals the most sophisticated financial management systems.

The Dance Begins

At the break of day, scout bees embark on a meticulous exploration of the vast expanse of flowers, diligently selecting those brimming with the most abundant nectar. Upon returning to the hive, they engage in a performance known as the "waggle dance," a ballet of information critical to the hive's collective financial planning.

Much like a meticulous financial planner, each bee contributes vital intelligence to the hive's overall strategy. The waggle dance's intensity and duration convey the richness of the nectar source, guiding other bees in making informed decisions about where to allocate their foraging efforts. To produce one pound of honey, honey bees must diligently gather nectar from nearly 2 million flowers [1], covering a staggering 90,000 miles, equivalent to three times around the Earth, in the process [2]. This underscores the imperative for efficiency and selectivity in their choices.

Resource Allocation: Nature's Budget

Informed by the scout bees, worker bees embark on foraging missions, visiting identified flowers and meticulously collecting nectar. This nectar, the hive's currency, is then brought back and deposited into the comb. Here unfolds another extraordinary dance—the allocation of resources.

Worker bees assess the hive's needs, factoring in considerations such as the number of developing larvae, current honey reserves, and the seasonal availability of flowers. Each drop of nectar is assigned a specific purpose—to nurture the brood, sustain the colony through lean times, or contribute to surplus stores. Managing resources wisely is imperative for the survival and prosperity of the hive, which typically comprises 20,000–60,000 bees and one queen [^3^].

Lesson 1: Precision in Purpose

In the honey bee's financial ballet, the lesson resonates clearly —every resource has a purpose, and its allocation is guided by a meticulous plan. This aligns profoundly with the principles of effective personal finance. Just as a bee carefully selects flowers and allocates nectar to meet specific needs, individuals can benefit from a purpose-driven approach to their finances.

Consider your income as the nectar of your endeavors. Before dispersing it, engage in your own "waggle dance" of financial planning. Communicate with your financial goals, signaling the direction in which your resources should flow. Whether nurturing your family, building a safety net, or investing for the future, each financial decision should align with a well-defined purpose. Notably, a mere 32% of Americans currently maintain a household budget [^4^], indicating that many are missing out on the benefits of planning and prioritizing their expenses.

Navigating the Financial Garden

Envision your financial landscape as a vibrant garden of opportunities, each representing a potential source of nectar. As the honey bee strategically selects flowers, be discerning in your choices. Identify income streams, investments, and expenditures aligned with your long-term objectives. Bees, critical to pollinating food crops that supply approximately 90% of the world's food, exemplify the significance of their role in the natural ecosystem. Analogously, your financial decisions impact not only your well-being but also that of your community and the planet.

Embarking on this journey inspired by the honey bee's financial ballet, let's internalize the first lesson—precision in purpose. The hive flourishes not through random foraging but through the deliberate allocation of resources. Similarly, your financial garden will bloom when tended with intention, and every budgetary decision becomes a step in the graceful ballet of financial well-being.

CHAPTER 2

"Sweet Savings: Lessons From The Honeycomb"

As the sun sets on the hive, casting a warm glow over the industrious colony, we delve into the heart of the honey bee's financial strategy—the art of sweet savings within the intricacies of the honeycomb. Within this hexagonal masterpiece, each cell tells a tale of diligent planning, efficient resource utilization, and a commitment to thriving through changing seasons.

The Honeycomb Symphony

In the honeycomb, a symphony of hexagons unfolds, each meticulously crafted to store honey, pollen, and nourish the hive. The bees, akin to savvy financial planners, understand the importance of building reserves during times of abundance to weather the inevitable lean periods. The intricate structure of the honeycomb itself serves as a testament to nature's optimal use of space and resources.

Research indicates that the hexagonal shape of the honeycomb cells is the most efficient way to store honey, minimizing the amount of wax needed and maximizing the amount of honey that can be stored. Bees use about 8 kg of nectar to produce 1 kg of wax, so by using less wax, they can save more honey. The honeycomb is also a remarkable example of structural engineering, as it can withstand high pressures and temperatures without collapsing.

The Nectar of Investment

The process of transforming collected nectar into honey mirrors the human financial journey of turning income into enduring wealth. Bees invest time and effort into dehydrating the nectar, reducing its water content to create a substance that can withstand the test of time. In the financial realm, wise investments similarly involve patience, strategic planning, and the ability to weather market fluctuations.

Like the honey bee's investment in creating honey, individuals can cultivate financial resilience by diversifying their investments. The honey bee doesn't put all its nectar in one cell, recognizing the importance of spreading risk. A well-balanced investment portfolio can weather economic fluctuations and provide stability over the long term.

Reports show that the global stock market capitalization reached a record high of $95 trillion in 2020, despite the pandemic-induced volatility. However, not all countries and sectors performed equally. For example, the US stock market gained 16% in 2020, while the UK market lost 14%. Investors who diversified their holdings across different regions and industries were able to reduce losses and increase gains.

Weathering the Financial Winter

As winter approaches, the honey bee faces a critical test of its savings strategy. The hive relies on stored honey to sustain itself when external nectar sources are scarce. Similarly, individuals must prepare for unforeseen challenges by building a robust financial safety net. Just as the honey bee meticulously calculates the amount of honey needed for survival, individuals can calculate their emergency fund requirements based on living expenses and potential financial risks.

A survey reveals that only 41% of Americans have a rainy day fund that can cover three months of expenses, while 28% have no emergency savings at all. This vulnerability to financial shocks highlights the importance of having an adequate emergency fund to cope with situations without resorting to high-interest debt or compromising long-term goals.

Lesson 2: The Power of Strategic Saving

The honey bee's approach to savings imparts a powerful lesson— strategic saving is the cornerstone of financial resilience. Each cell in the honeycomb represents a carefully stored resource, serving as a lifeline during lean times. Similarly, individuals can cultivate financial security by adopting a disciplined approach to saving.

Consider your savings as the honeycomb of your financial hive. Allocate funds to different "cells"—an emergency fund, investments, retirement savings—each serving a specific purpose. Diversify your financial cells, just as the honey bee diversifies its honey storage, to ensure a well-rounded and resilient financial portfolio.

Money Saved is Money Earned

Remember, money saved is money earned. If we spend everything we earn, we cannot plan for a future. Saving is a habit, and it takes time to build this habit. Let's consider two individuals —one earning more but spending lavishly without saving, and the other earning less but diligently saving and investing. In the long run, the person earning less may lead a better lifestyle as the money multiplies, ensuring a comfortable retirement. This example underscores the significance of saving as a habit for long-term financial well-being.

Reports indicate that India has one of the highest savings rates in the world, with a gross national savings rate of 28.3% of GDP in 2020. This reflects the traditional culture of saving and investing among Indians, prioritizing long-term goals such as education, marriage, and retirement over short-term consumption. However, there's a need to improve financial literacy and diversify savings across different asset classes, as reliance on fixed income products like bank deposits and insurance policies is prevalent.

Join me in the next chapter as we explore the collaborative spirit within the hive and uncover how communal financial strategies contribute to the hive's overall success.

CHAPTER 3:

"Collaborative Prosperity: Insights From The Hive Community"

As we venture deeper into the intricate dynamics of hive living, we unveil the collaborative nature that defines the honey bee community. In this chapter, we'll explore how the hive's communal spirit offers valuable insights into the potential benefits of collaborative financial strategies for individuals within a community.

The Hive as a Collective Entity

Within the hive, each bee plays a distinct role, contributing to the greater good of the community. Worker bees collaborate seamlessly, sharing responsibilities such as foraging, nursing, and hive maintenance. The hive operates as a collective entity, and its prosperity relies on the cooperation of its members.

The honey bee colony exhibits a remarkable degree of self-organization, coordination, and collective intelligence, despite the limited cognitive abilities of individual bees. The colony acts as a "superorganism", a term coined by the biologist William Morton Wheeler in 1911, to describe a group of organisms that function as a single unit.

Financial Collaboration in Human Communities

Drawing parallels between hive living and human communities, we find inspiration for collaborative financial strategies. In the hive, bees work together to achieve common goals, recognizing that collective effort leads to greater overall success. Similarly, individuals within a community can harness the power of collaboration for financial well-being.

Collaborative consumption, also known as the sharing economy, is a growing trend that enables people to access goods and services through peer-to-peer platforms, rather than owning them. The global sharing economy is expected to grow from $15 billion in 2014 to $335 billion in 2025, driven by factors such as digitalization, environmental awareness, and social connectedness. Examples of collaborative consumption include Airbnb, Uber, and Kickstarter.

Group Investments and Resource Pooling

Just as bees pool resources for the hive's benefit, community members can explore group investments and resource pooling. Collaborative ventures, such as investment clubs or community funds, allow individuals to combine their financial strength. This approach enables shared decision-making, risk mitigation, and the potential for greater returns.

Investment clubs are groups of people who pool their money and invest collectively, usually in stocks or bonds. Investment clubs have several benefits, such as learning from each other, diversifying risk, and achieving higher returns than individual investors. Investment clubs tend to have a long-term perspective, a disciplined approach, and a focus on value investing.

Learning from the Bee's Communication

The honey bee community relies on intricate communication through dances, pheromones, and signals. Likewise, effective financial collaboration in human communities requires clear communication and transparency. Sharing insights, goals, and challenges ensures that everyone is aligned, contributing to the success of collaborative financial initiatives.

The honey bee's waggle dance is a sophisticated form of communication that conveys information about the direction, distance, and quality of a food source. The waggle dance enables the colony to optimize its foraging efficiency, allocate resources effectively, and adapt to changing environments. The waggle dance is also a form of collective decision-making, as the bees can influence and be influenced by the dances of others.

Strengthening the Financial Ecosystem

In the hive, bees recognize the interdependence of their roles in maintaining the overall health of the colony. Similarly, within a community, individuals can strengthen the financial ecosystem by supporting one another. Mentorship, knowledge sharing, and collaborative initiatives contribute to the collective financial well-being of the community.

Financial inclusion is the access and use of formal financial services by all segments of society, especially the poor and marginalized. Financial inclusion is essential for reducing poverty, promoting economic growth, and enhancing social cohesion. Financial education, innovation, and regulation are key factors in advancing financial inclusion.

Lesson 3: Community Collaboration for Financial Resilience

The honey bee's hive is a testament to the power of community collaboration, showcasing how collective efforts lead to prosperity. Individuals can adopt similar principles within their communities, fostering collaboration for financial resilience. By pooling resources, sharing knowledge, and supporting one another's financial goals, communities can navigate challenges more effectively and achieve greater long-term prosperity.

Join me in the next chapter as we delve into the hive's ability to adapt to change and explore how resilience in the face of challenges can inspire robust financial strategies for individuals.

Comparing the Honey Bee Colony with Household, Society, and Country

The honey bee colony can be compared with different levels of human organization, such as household, society, and country. At each level, we can learn from the savings and investment perspective of the hive.

Household

A household is a basic unit of human living, consisting of one or more people who share a dwelling and resources. A household can learn from the honey bee colony how to manage its income and expenses, save for the future, and invest wisely.

- A household can emulate the honey bee's precision in purpose, allocating its income to different categories, such as food, rent, utilities, education, health, and entertainment. A household can also set aside a portion of its income for savings and investments, following the honey bee's example of creating honey reserves.

- A household can emulate the honey bee's adaptation and flexibility, adjusting its spending and saving habits according to the changing circumstances and needs. A household can also prepare for unforeseen events, such as job loss, illness, or natural disasters, by having an emergency fund, following the honey bee's example of weathering the winter.

- A household can emulate the honey bee's community collaboration, joining forces with other households to pool resources, share knowledge, and support each other's financial goals. A household can also participate in collaborative consumption, such as renting, sharing, or swapping goods and services, following the honey bee's example of collective efficiency.

Society

A society is a group of people who share a common culture, values, and norms. A society can learn from the honey bee colony how to foster social cohesion, economic development, and environmental sustainability.

- A society can emulate the honey bee's precision in purpose, allocating its resources to different sectors, such as education, health, infrastructure, and security. A society can also set aside a portion of its resources for savings and investments, following the honey bee's example of creating honey reserves.

- A society can emulate the honey bee's adaptation and flexibility, adapting its policies and programs according to the changing needs and challenges of its members. A society can also prepare for unforeseen events, such as pandemics, wars, or natural disasters, by having a contingency fund, following the honey bee's example of weathering the winter.

- A society can emulate the honey bee's community collaboration, promoting cooperation and solidarity among its members, as well as with other societies. A society can also participate in collaborative consumption, such as trading, donating, or volunteering goods and services, following the honey bee's example of collective efficiency.

Country

A country is a political entity that has sovereignty over a territory and population. A country can learn from the honey bee colony how to maintain its national security, economic growth, and international relations.

- A country can emulate the honey bee's precision in purpose, allocating its budget to different functions, such as defense, public services, and debt repayment. A country can also set aside a portion of its budget for savings and investments, following the honey bee's example of creating honey reserves.

- A country can emulate the honey bee's adaptation and flexibility, adjusting its fiscal and monetary policies according to the changing economic conditions and demands. A country can also prepare for unforeseen events, such as recessions, inflation, or currency crises, by having a foreign exchange reserve, following the honey bee's example of weathering the winter.

- A country can emulate the honey bee's community collaboration, establishing alliances and partnerships with other countries to enhance trade, security, and diplomacy. A country can also participate in collaborative consumption, such as providing or receiving aid, loans, or grants, following the honey bee's example of collective efficiency.

CHAPTER 4:

"Nectar Of Investments: Building Wealth Bee-Style"

In the buzzing realm of the honey bee, the art of investing takes center stage as bees diligently gather nectar from diverse sources. This chapter delves into the parallel universe of bee-style wealth building, drawing insights from the strategic investment choices of these industrious pollinators.

Diverse Foraging for Financial Abundance

Honey bees showcase a remarkable diversity in their foraging patterns, selecting nectar from a wide array of flowers. Similarly, individuals can emulate this strategy by diversifying their investment portfolio. The bee's approach recognizes that different sources contribute unique benefits, fostering resilience in the face of changing economic landscapes.

One of the benefits of diversification is that it reduces the overall risk of the portfolio, as different assets tend to react differently to market fluctuations. For example, stocks and bonds often have an inverse relationship, meaning that when one goes up, the other goes down. By holding both stocks and bonds, investors can balance out the volatility of their portfolio and smooth out their returns over time.

Another benefit of diversification is that it increases the opportunities for growth, as different assets tend to perform better in different economic scenarios. For example, growth stocks and real estate tend to do well in periods of economic expansion, while value stocks and commodities tend to do well in periods of economic contraction. By holding a mix of assets, investors can capture the upside potential of various sectors and regions.

According to a study, a diversified portfolio of 60% stocks and 40% bonds had an average annual return of 8.6% and a standard deviation (a measure of risk) of 10.6% from 1926 to 2018 1. In contrast, a portfolio of 100% stocks had an average annual return of 10.1% and a standard deviation of 20.1%, while a portfolio of 100% bonds had an average annual return of 5.3% and a standard deviation of 5.7%. This shows that diversification can improve the risk-return trade-off of a portfolio.

The Wisdom of Pollination

As bees cross-pollinate various flowers, they play a vital role in the ecosystem's health. In the financial landscape, strategic investments can also serve as agents of cross-pollination. By allocating funds across different asset classes—stocks, bonds, real estate, and more—individuals can create a robust and interconnected investment portfolio that thrives in diverse market conditions.

One of the advantages of cross-pollination is that it enhances the efficiency of the portfolio, as different assets tend to have different correlations with each other. Correlation is a measure of how closely two assets move together, ranging from -1 (perfectly negative) to 1 (perfectly positive). A low or negative correlation means that two assets tend to move in opposite directions, while a high or positive correlation means that two assets tend to move in the same direction.

By combining assets with low or negative correlations, investors can reduce the overall volatility of their portfolio and increase their chances of achieving positive returns in any market environment. For example, stocks and bonds have a low correlation of 0.1, while stocks and gold have a negative correlation of -0.1 2. By holding both stocks and bonds, or stocks and gold, investors can hedge against the risk of a stock market crash.

Another advantage of cross-pollination is that it expands the possibilities for growth, as different assets tend to have different drivers of returns. For example, stocks are driven by earnings growth, dividends, and valuation changes, while bonds are driven by interest rates, credit quality, and inflation expectations. By holding a variety of assets, investors can benefit from multiple sources of returns and diversify their income streams.

According to a report, a global portfolio of 50% stocks, 40% bonds, and 10% alternative assets (such as real estate, commodities, and hedge funds) had an average annual return of 7.9% and a standard deviation of 9.5% from 2000 to 2019 3. In contrast, a portfolio of 100% US stocks had an average annual return of 6.1% and a standard deviation of 15.3%, while a portfolio of 100% US bonds had an average annual return of 4.9% and a standard deviation of 3.6%. This shows that cross-pollination can enhance the performance and diversification of a portfolio.

Nurturing the Financial Hive

Just as bees nurture their hive with a variety of nectar, individuals can nurture their financial well-being by considering a mix of investment options. From low-risk, stable investments to ventures with higher growth potential, a well-balanced investment strategy ensures sustained prosperity over time.

One of the factors to consider when choosing investment options is the risk-return profile of each asset. Risk is the uncertainty or variability of returns, while return is the reward or income from investing. Generally, there is a positive relationship between risk and return, meaning that higher-risk assets tend to offer higher returns, while lower-risk assets tend to offer lower returns.

By understanding the risk-return profile of each asset, investors can select the appropriate mix of investments that matches their risk tolerance, time horizon, and financial goals. For example, investors who are risk-averse, have a short-term time horizon, or need a steady income may prefer low-risk, stable investments, such as money market funds, certificates of deposit, or treasury bills. Investors who are risk-tolerant, have a long-term time horizon, or seek capital appreciation may prefer high-risk, growth-oriented investments, such as stocks, real estate, or venture capital.

Another factor to consider when choosing investment options is the tax implications of each asset. Tax is the amount of money that investors have to pay to the government on their investment income or capital gains. Different assets have different tax treatments, depending on the type, amount, and duration of the income or gain.

By understanding the tax implications of each asset, investors can optimize their after-tax returns and minimize their tax liability. For example, investors who are in a high tax bracket or have a large taxable income may prefer tax-advantaged investments, such as municipal bonds, Roth IRAs, or 401(k) plans. Investors who are in a low tax bracket or have a small taxable income may prefer tax-efficient investments, such as index funds, exchange-traded funds, or qualified dividends.

Risk Mitigation Bee-Style

Bees understand the importance of risk mitigation in their foraging pursuits. They gauge factors like weather conditions, flower availability, and potential threats. Similarly, investors can adopt a bee-style approach by conducting thorough research, staying informed about market trends, and diversifying their investments to mitigate risks effectively.

One of the types of risk that investors face is market risk, which is the risk of losing money due to movements in the market prices of assets. Market risk can be caused by various factors, such as economic cycles, interest rate changes, political events, or natural disasters. Market risk affects all assets to some degree, but some are more sensitive than others.

By conducting thorough research, investors can assess the market risk of each asset and determine the appropriate level of exposure. For example, investors who are concerned about a recession may reduce their exposure to cyclical stocks, which are stocks that tend to perform well in periods of economic growth and poorly in periods of economic decline. Investors who are concerned about inflation may increase their exposure to inflation-protected securities, which are bonds that adjust their principal and interest payments based on changes in the inflation rate.

Another type of risk that investors face is specific risk, which is the risk of losing money due to factors that affect a particular asset or a group of assets. Specific risk can be caused by various factors, such as company performance, industry competition, regulatory changes, or technological innovations. Specific risk affects only a subset of assets, and can be diversified away by holding a large number of assets.

By staying informed about market trends, investors can identify and avoid the specific risk of each asset and sector. For example, investors who are aware of the rise of electric vehicles may avoid investing in oil and gas companies, which may face lower demand and profitability in the future. Investors who are aware of the growth of e-commerce may avoid investing in brick-and-mortar retailers, which may face higher competition and lower sales in the future.

Time as the Bee's Ally

The honey bee's investment in nectar requires patience as they transform raw materials into honey over time. Individuals can learn from this patient approach and recognize the power of long-term investments. Just as honey accumulates drop by drop, consistent contributions to investment portfolios can lead to significant wealth accumulation over the years.

One of the benefits of long-term investing is that it allows investors to take advantage of compound interest, which is the interest earned on both the principal and the accumulated interest. Compound interest can have a dramatic effect on the growth of an investment over time, as the interest is reinvested and earns more interest.

By making consistent contributions to their investment portfolios, investors can increase the amount of compound interest they earn and accelerate the growth of their wealth. For example, an investor who invests $10,000 at an annual interest rate of 8% and makes no additional contributions will have $46,610 after 20 years. However, an investor who invests $10,000 at the same interest rate and makes additional contributions of $100 per month will have $98,846 after 20 years.

Another benefit of long-term investing is that it allows investors to benefit from the historical performance of the market, which tends to rise over time despite occasional fluctuations. The market is influenced by various factors, such as earnings, dividends, valuations, and expectations, which can cause the

Exercise: Diversify Your Financial Nectar

Objective: To understand the concept of diversification in investment and its potential benefits.

Instructions:
1. Research and Identify Investment Options: Research different investment options available, such as stocks, bonds, real estate, and mutual funds. Understand the basic principles and risks associated with each.

2. Allocate Your Financial Nectar: Imagine your financial resources as the nectar collected by a honey bee. Allocate a percentage of your "nectar" to different

investment options based on your risk tolerance, financial goals, and time horizon. For example, if you have $10,000 of "nectar" and you are a conservative investor with a long-term goal of retirement, you may allocate 40% to bonds, 30% to stocks, 20% to real estate, and 10% to mutual funds.

3. Create a Diversified Portfolio: Build a diversified portfolio by distributing your allocated funds across various investment categories. Consider the bee's approach of gathering nectar from different flowers to create a resilient and varied source of sustenance. For example, if you allocated 40% to bonds, you may choose to invest in a mix of government and corporate bonds with different maturities and interest rates. If you allocated 30% to stocks, you may choose to invest in a mix of large-cap and small-cap stocks from different industries and countries.

4. Monitor and Assess: Keep track of your investments and monitor their performance over time. Reflect on how diversification has impacted the stability and growth of your portfolio. You can use online tools or apps to track your portfolio's value, returns, and risk. You can also compare your portfolio's performance with relevant benchmarks, such as market indices or average returns of similar portfolios.

5. Lesson Learned: Diversification Lesson: The Bee's Wisdom in Wealth Building

Key Takeaways:

- Mitigating Risks: Diversification helps spread risks across different assets, reducing the impact of poor performance in any single investment. By holding a variety of assets, you can reduce the volatility of your portfolio and protect your wealth from market downturns.

- Adaptability: Just as bees adapt to changing conditions by foraging from various flowers, diversifying investments allows for adaptability in different market scenarios. By holding a variety of assets, you can benefit from the opportunities and avoid the pitfalls of different economic cycles, interest rate changes, and geopolitical events.

- Resilience: A diversified portfolio can weather economic fluctuations better, reflecting the bee's ability to thrive despite varying environmental factors. By holding a variety of assets, you can maintain a steady income stream and preserve your purchasing power in the face of inflation and currency fluctuations.

- Long-Term Growth: By consistently contributing to a well-diversified portfolio, individuals can experience steady and long-term wealth accumulation. By holding a variety of assets, you can benefit from the power of compound interest and the historical performance of the market, which tends to rise over time.

Reflection Questions:

- How did diversifying your "financial nectar" impact the overall performance and stability of your investment portfolio?

- What parallels did you observe between the bee's approach to foraging and your strategy in selecting diverse investment options?

- In what ways can the lessons from the honey bee's diversification strategy be applied to your personal financial planning for long-term success?

Remember, just as the honey bee diligently diversifies its nectar sources for the prosperity of the hive, diversifying your investments can contribute to your financial well-being and

SHAMSUD ZAMAN

resilience.

CHAPTER 5:

"The Buzz Of Entrepreneurship" Lessons From The Queen Bee

I n the heart of the hive, a remarkable leader takes center stage —the queen bee. As the embodiment of reproductive prowess and the focal point of the hive's entrepreneurial endeavors, the queen bee imparts invaluable lessons on the entrepreneurial spirit. In this chapter, we'll delve into the hive's bustling world to extract insights on how individuals can channel the drive of the queen bee to create opportunities for financial growth.

The Queen Bee's Royal Role

The queen bee stands as the epicenter of the hive's entrepreneurial activities. Her role goes beyond mere reproduction; she serves as a driving force for expansion, innovation, and sustained growth. Much like a successful entrepreneur, the queen bee exhibits visionary leadership and a keen understanding of the hive's needs. One of the most successful entrepreneurs who exemplifies the queen bee's royal role is Jeff Bezos, the founder and CEO of Amazon. Bezos started Amazon as an online bookstore in 1994, but soon expanded it into a global e-commerce giant that sells everything from books to groceries to cloud computing services. Bezos has a vision of making Amazon the "everything store" that can deliver anything to anyone, anywhere, anytime. Bezos also understands the needs of his customers and constantly innovates to meet them. For example, he introduced the Kindle e-reader, the Prime membership program, and the Alexa voice assistant to enhance the customer experience and loyalty. Bezos also leads other ventures, such as Blue Origin, a space exploration company, and The Washington Post, a newspaper. Bezos is widely regarded as one of the most influential and visionary entrepreneurs of our time[12]

Another example of a queen bee leader is Kiran Mazumdar-Shaw, the founder and chairperson of Biocon, India's largest biopharmaceutical company. Mazumdar-Shaw started Biocon in 1978 as a small enzyme manufacturing firm, with a seed capital of only $500. She faced many challenges and barriers, such as lack of funding, credibility, and infrastructure, as well as gender discrimination in a male-dominated industry. However, she persevered and grew Biocon into a global leader in biotechnology, with a presence in over 120 countries and a market value of over $5 billion. Mazumdar-Shaw is also a pioneer in social entrepreneurship, investing in health care, education, and environmental initiatives. She is widely recognized as one of the most influential and successful women entrepreneurs in the world[34]

Fostering Innovation in the Hive

Entrepreneurship thrives on innovation, and the hive is no exception. Queen bees play a pivotal role in fostering innovation by leading the swarm to new foraging grounds, adapting to environmental changes, and optimizing resource utilization. Their entrepreneurial spirit lies in the ability to identify opportunities for growth and guide the hive towards prosperity.

One of the most successful entrepreneurs who exemplifies the queen bee's role in fostering innovation is Elon Musk, the founder and CEO of Tesla, SpaceX, and Neuralink. Musk is known for his ambitious and groundbreaking projects that aim to revolutionize transportation, energy, and human potential. Musk founded Tesla in 2003 to produce electric vehicles that are sustainable, affordable, and high-performance. He also founded SpaceX in

2002 to develop reusable rockets and spacecraft that can enable human colonization of Mars. He also founded Neuralink in 2016 to create brain-computer interfaces that can enhance human cognition and communication. Musk is driven by a passion for solving the world's biggest problems and creating a positive impact on humanity[56]

Another example of a queen bee innovator is Angela Merkel, the chancellor of Germany and the leader of the European Union. Merkel is known for her pragmatic and rational approach to governance, as well as her ability to navigate complex and challenging situations. Merkel has led Germany and the EU through multiple crises, such as the global financial crisis, the European debt crisis, the refugee crisis, the Brexit referendum, and the Covid-19 pandemic. She has also championed innovation and sustainability, promoting renewable energy, digital transformation, and climate action. Merkel is widely respected as one of the most powerful and influential leaders in the world[78]

Collaboration and Delegation

Successful entrepreneurs understand the significance of collaboration and effective delegation. The queen bee excels in both aspects, collaborating with worker bees to execute hive tasks and delegating responsibilities efficiently. This collaborative approach ensures that the hive operates as a cohesive unit, maximizing productivity and achieving collective goals.

One of the most successful entrepreneurs who exemplifies the queen bee's role in collaboration and delegation is Richard Branson, the founder and chairman of the Virgin Group. Branson started his first business, a magazine called Student, at the age of 16. He then launched Virgin Records, a record label that signed artists such as the Sex Pistols, the Rolling Stones, and Madonna. He later expanded the Virgin brand into various sectors, such as airlines, hotels, telecommunications, and space tourism. Branson attributes his success to his ability to build and lead teams that share his vision and values. He also empowers his employees to make decisions and take risks, creating a culture of innovation and entrepreneurship. Branson believes that collaboration and delegation are essential for achieving business and social goals.

Another example of a queen bee collaborator and delegator is Ratan Tata, the former chairman of Tata Group, India's largest conglomerate. Tata joined the family business in 1962 and became its chairman in 1991. He transformed Tata Group from a domestic company into a global powerhouse, with over 100 operating companies in various industries, such as steel, automobiles, software, and hospitality. He also led the acquisitions of iconic brands, such as Jaguar Land Rover, Tetley, and Corus. Tata is known for his humble and ethical leadership style, as well as his ability to inspire and mentor his employees and successors. He is also a philanthropist, donating billions of dollars to various causes, such as education, health, and environment. Tata is widely admired as one of the most respected and successful business leaders in the world.

Risk-Taking and Swarm Ventures

Queen bees epitomize the art of calculated risk-taking. When the hive population grows, the queen encourages a swarm to venture into the unknown, seeking new territories and resources. Entrepreneurs can draw inspiration from this risk-taking mentality, understanding that calculated risks are essential for exploring new opportunities and fostering financial growth.

One of the most successful entrepreneurs who exemplifies the queen bee's role in risk-taking and swarm ventures is Jack Ma, the co-founder and former executive chairman of Alibaba Group. Ma started Alibaba in 1999 as an online marketplace that connects Chinese suppliers with global buyers. He faced many challenges and risks, such as lack of funding, fierce competition, and regulatory hurdles. However, he persevered and grew Alibaba into one of the world's largest e-commerce platforms, with over 800 million active users and over $1 trillion in annual gross merchandise volume. Ma also launched other ventures, such as Alipay, an online payment service, Ant Group, a financial technology company, and Taobao, a consumer-to-consumer marketplace. Ma is known for his entrepreneurial spirit and his willingness to take bold and unconventional risks.

Another example of a queen bee risk-taker and swarm venturer is Anne Wojcicki, the co-founder and CEO of 23andMe, a personal genomics and biotechnology company. Wojcicki started 23andMe in 2006 with the vision of empowering people to access and understand their own genetic information. She faced many challenges and risks, such as raising capital, overcoming technical hurdles, and complying with regulatory standards. However, she persisted and grew 23andMe into a leading company in the field of direct-to-consumer genetic testing, with over 12 million customers and over $900 million in funding. Wojcicki also launched other ventures, such as Breakthrough.com, an online therapy platform, and Loon, a balloon-powered internet service. Wojcicki is recognized as one of the most innovative and influential entrepreneurs in the world.

Nurturing the Succession Pipeline

Entrepreneurial success often relies on effective succession planning. Queen bees, too, focus on nurturing a successor—the next queen. This deliberate approach ensures the continuity of leadership and the hive's long-term success. Entrepreneurs can learn from this strategy by investing in mentorship and preparing the next generation for leadership roles within their ventures.

One of the most successful entrepreneurs who exemplifies the queen bee's role in nurturing the succession pipeline is Indra Nooyi, the former CEO and chairman of PepsiCo. Nooyi joined PepsiCo in 1994 and became its CEO in 2006. She led the company through a period of transformation and growth, expanding its product portfolio, increasing its global presence, and enhancing its social and environmental performance. She also mentored and groomed her successor, Ramon Laguarta, who became the CEO in 2018 and the chairman in 2019. Nooyi is widely respected for her leadership and her commitment to developing the next generation of leaders.

Another example of a queen bee nurturer and mentor is Arianna Huffington, the co-founder and former editor-in-chief of The Huffington Post, a leading online news and opinion platform. Huffington started The Huffington Post in 2005 with the mission of providing a voice for people who were not represented in the mainstream media. She led the company to become one of the most

Exercise: Unleash Your Inner Entrepreneurial Bee

Objective: To explore and apply the entrepreneurial lessons inspired by the queen bee, fostering a mindset of innovation, collaboration, and calculated risk-taking.

Instructions:

Identify Your Financial Hive:

Reflect on your financial goals and aspirations. Imagine your financial journey as a hive, with the potential for growth and prosperity. Write down your short-term and long-term objectives, such as saving for a vacation, buying a house, starting a business, or retiring comfortably. Think about how your current income, expenses, assets, and liabilities affect your ability to achieve your goals. Also, consider your personal values, interests, and passions, and how they influence your financial decisions.

Embrace Innovation:

Identify one aspect of your financial life that could benefit from innovation. It could be related to earning, saving, investing, or any other financial endeavor. For example, you could explore new ways to increase your income, such as starting a side hustle, asking for a raise, or switching careers. You could also look for creative ways to save more money, such as cutting down unnecessary expenses, automating your savings, or using apps that round up your purchases and invest the change. You could also seek new opportunities to grow your money, such as investing in the stock market, real estate, or cryptocurrencies.

Brainstorm creative ideas on how to approach this aspect differently. Consider how the queen bee would seek new foraging grounds to optimize resources. For example, if you want to invest in the stock market, you could research different types of stocks, such as growth, value, dividend, or blue-chip stocks. You could also diversify your portfolio by investing in different sectors, such as technology, health care, or consumer goods. You could also use online tools, such as robo-advisors, stock screeners, or trading platforms, to help you make informed decisions.

Foster Collaboration:

Recognize the importance of collaboration in your financial journey. Identify individuals or resources that can contribute to your goals. For example, you could find a mentor who has achieved similar goals and can offer guidance and advice. You could also consult a financial advisor who can help you create a financial plan and recommend suitable products and services. You could also join a community of like-minded people who can provide support, feedback, and accountability.

Reach out to a mentor, financial advisor, or potential collaborators. Discuss ideas, seek advice, and build a collaborative network. For example, you could ask your mentor about their challenges and successes, and learn from their experiences. You could also ask your financial advisor about the best strategies and options for your situation, and follow their recommendations. You could also share your ideas and progress with your community, and get their input and encouragement.

Take Calculated Risks:

Entrepreneurship involves calculated risks. Identify a financial opportunity or investment that aligns with your goals. For example, you could start a small business based on your skills or passions, such as selling handmade crafts, offering online tutoring, or blogging. You could also invest in a promising company or industry that has the potential to grow in the future, such as renewable energy, biotechnology, or e-commerce.

Evaluate the potential risks and rewards. Develop a strategy to mitigate risks while maximizing the potential for financial growth. For example, you could do a SWOT analysis to identify the strengths, weaknesses, opportunities, and threats of your opportunity or investment. You could also do a cost-benefit analysis to compare the expected costs and benefits of your decision. You could also set a budget and a timeline for your project or investment, and monitor your performance and progress.

Invest in Succession Planning:

Consider your financial legacy and long-term goals. Reflect on how you can nurture the next phase of your financial journey. For example, you could create a will or a trust to ensure your assets are distributed according to your wishes. You could also designate beneficiaries for your accounts and policies, and update them regularly. You could also plan for your retirement, such as saving in a retirement account, choosing a retirement date, and deciding where and how you want to live.

Identify individuals, whether family members, mentees, or partners, who can benefit from your insights and contribute to the continuity of your financial success. For example, you could teach your children or grandchildren about financial literacy, such as budgeting, saving, and investing. You could also mentor someone who wants to follow your footsteps, and share your knowledge and skills. You could also partner with someone who shares your vision, and collaborate on a project or a venture.

Lesson Learned:

Entrepreneurial Mindset Lesson: Unleashing Your Inner Queen Bee

Key Takeaways:

Innovation Drives Growth: Like the queen bee exploring new foraging grounds, embracing innovation in your financial approach can lead to opportunities for growth and prosperity. By thinking outside the box and trying new things, you can increase your income, save more money, and grow your wealth.

Collaboration Amplifies Impact: Collaborating with others enhances your financial capabilities. Seek and build partnerships that can contribute to the collective success of your financial hive. By learning from others, seeking professional help, and joining a community, you can gain valuable insights, support, and resources.

Calculated Risks Lead to Rewards: Taking calculated risks is an inherent part of entrepreneurship. Evaluate opportunities, weigh the risks, and be prepared to take strategic leaps for financial rewards. By doing your research, analyzing your options, and developing a plan, you can minimize the downside and maximize the upside of your decisions.

Succession Planning Ensures Continuity: Nurturing the next generation of financial leaders ensures the continuity of success. Invest in mentorship and share your financial insights to create a lasting impact. By planning for your legacy, teaching others, and partnering with others, you can ensure your financial goals are achieved and sustained.

Reflection Questions:

How did embracing innovation in one aspect of your financial life impact your perspective and potential opportunities?

What collaborations did you initiate, and how do you foresee them contributing to your financial success?

Describe a calculated risk you took in your financial journey. What were the outcomes, and what did you learn from the experience?

How can you contribute to the financial success of others, embodying the queen bee's approach to succession planning?

Remember, by unleashing your inner entrepreneurial bee, you can cultivate a mindset that propels you toward financial growth and prosperity.

Here I am sharing a form to manage your earning, spending, and investing. Here is a possible template:

Monthly Financial Tracker

Category	Amount	Percentage
Earning	₹	%
Spending	₹	%
Investing	₹	%
Total	₹	100%

Investment Breakdown

Type of Investment	Amount	Percentage
Stocks	₹	%
Bonds	₹	%

Real Estate	₹	%
Mutual Funds	₹	%
Index Funds	₹	%
Exchange-Traded Funds	₹	%
Options	₹	%
Other	₹	%
Total	₹	100%

Instructions:

Fill in the amount of money you invest in each type of investment each month in the corresponding cells. For example, if you invest ₹5,000 in stocks, ₹3,000 in bonds, ₹1,000 in real estate, and ₹1,000 in mutual funds, enter those amounts in the table.

Calculate the percentage of each type of investment by dividing the amount by the total and multiplying by 100. For example, if you invest ₹5,000 in stocks, ₹3,000 in bonds, ₹1,000 in real estate, and ₹1,000 in mutual funds, the percentages are 50%, 30%, 10%, and 10%, respectively.

Use the table to track your investment portfolio and goals

Remember, by breaking down your investment part into different types of investment, you can gain more insight and clarity over your investment strategy and performance.

Here are some of the best personal finance apps and websites from India and across the globe:

- Money View: This is an app that helps you track your income, expenses, and investments by reading your transactional SMS messages. You can also check your bank balances, get bill reminders, and find savings opportunities[1]
- Mint: This is a website and app that helps you create and manage your budget, track your spending, and monitor your credit score. You can also link your bank accounts, cards, and investments to get a holistic view of your finances[2]
- Zoho Books: This is a website and app that helps you manage your business accounting online. You can send invoices, record expenses, track inventory, and generate reports. You can also integrate with other Zoho products and third-party apps[3]
- Goodbudget: This is an app that helps you manage your personal budget using the envelope system. You can allocate your income to different categories, such as groceries, rent, and entertainment, and track your spending. You can also sync your budget with your partner or family[4]

CHAPTER 6:

"Mindful Spending: Navigating The Flower Patch Of Consumer Choices"

In the intricate dance of nature, honey bees exhibit a remarkable discernment when foraging for nectar. They carefully select flowers that offer the most value and sustenance for the hive. In this chapter, we'll draw inspiration from the honey bee's selective foraging habits and explore the concept of mindful spending. By navigating the vast flower patch of consumer choices with intention and awareness, individuals can cultivate a financial approach that aligns with their values and long-term goals.

The Art of Selective Foraging

Honey bees don't mindlessly visit every flower in the garden; instead, they prioritize those with the richest nectar. Similarly, mindful spending involves making intentional choices about where to allocate financial resources. By embracing the principle of selective foraging, individuals can enhance their financial well-being and satisfaction.

Selective foraging means spending money on things that truly matter to you, and avoiding spending on things that don't. It means being conscious of your needs versus your wants, and choosing quality over quantity. It means spending less on things that don't add value to your life, and spending more on things that do. It means spending in a way that reflects your personal values, goals, and priorities.

For example, you may choose to spend more money on organic food, because you value your health and the environment. You may choose to spend less money on clothes, because you don't care about fashion trends and prefer a minimalist wardrobe. You may choose to spend money on experiences, such as travel, education, or hobbies, because they enrich your life and make you happy. You may choose to save money for your retirement, because you want to secure your future and enjoy your golden years.

Selective foraging helps you optimize your financial resources and achieve your financial goals. It also helps you avoid unnecessary debt, stress, and clutter. It helps you live within your means, and enjoy the fruits of your labor.

Cultivating Financial Awareness

Foraging honey bees are acutely aware of their surroundings, attuned to the nuances of each flower. Likewise, mindful spending requires heightened financial awareness. This entails understanding personal spending patterns, distinguishing between needs and wants, and recognizing the impact of financial choices on long-term goals.

Financial awareness means being mindful of your income and expenses, and tracking them regularly. It means knowing how much money you earn, how much money you spend, and how much money you save or invest. It means being aware of where your money goes, and how it aligns with your budget and your goals.

Financial awareness also means being mindful of your emotions and motivations, and how they affect your spending behavior.

It means being aware of your spending triggers, such as stress, boredom, peer pressure, or social media. It means being aware of your spending habits, such as impulse buying, retail therapy, or overspending. It means being aware of your spending values, such as convenience, comfort, or status.

Financial awareness helps you make informed and intentional financial decisions. It also helps you identify and change any negative or unhealthy spending patterns. It helps you develop a positive and healthy relationship with money, and use it as a tool to improve your life.

The Impact of Consumer Choices

Just as honey bees' choices influence the hive's prosperity, individual spending decisions have a profound impact on personal financial health. Mindful spending involves evaluating the value of each purchase, considering its alignment with overall goals, and acknowledging the potential ripple effects on savings and investments.

Evaluating the value of each purchase means considering the benefits and costs of each spending decision. It means asking yourself questions such as: Do I really need this? Do I really want this? Will this make me happy? How long will this last? Is this worth the price? Is there a better alternative? How will this affect my budget? How will this affect my goals?

Considering the alignment with overall goals means ensuring that each spending decision supports your short-term and long-term financial objectives. It means asking yourself questions such as: How does this fit into my budget? How does this fit into my savings plan? How does this fit into my investment strategy? How does this fit into my retirement plan? How does this fit into my life plan?

Acknowledging the potential ripple effects on savings and investments means being aware of the opportunity cost and the compound interest of each spending decision. It means asking yourself questions such as: What else could I do with this money? How much could I save or earn if I invested this money instead? How will this affect my future income and wealth? How will this affect my financial security and freedom?

Evaluating the value, considering the alignment, and acknowledging the ripple effects of each purchase helps you spend your money wisely and effectively. It also helps you avoid unnecessary or regrettable purchases, and maximize your financial potential.

Budgeting as the Financial Garden Map

A bee navigates the flower patch with a purpose, and individuals can approach spending with a similar sense of direction. Budgeting serves as the financial garden map, guiding spending decisions and ensuring that financial resources are allocated efficiently. Mindful budgeting allows for intentional distribution of income, minimizing financial waste.

Budgeting means creating and following a plan for your income and expenses, based on your goals and priorities. It means allocating a specific amount of money for each spending category, such as housing, food, transportation, entertainment, etc. It means tracking your spending and comparing it to your budget, and making adjustments as needed.

Budgeting also means setting aside a portion of your income for savings and investments, based on your goals and risk tolerance. It means creating an emergency fund, a retirement fund, and other specific funds for your short-term and long-term objectives. It means investing your money in a diversified portfolio, and monitoring its performance and growth.

Budgeting helps you manage your money effectively and efficiently. It also helps you live within your means, avoid debt, and build wealth. It helps you achieve your financial goals, and enjoy your financial journey.

Lesson 6: Mindful Spending for Financial Pollination

In the honey bee's world, selective foraging ensures the hive's prosperity. Similarly, individuals can adopt mindful spending practices to pollinate their financial goals. By cultivating awareness, making intentional choices, and aligning spending with overarching objectives, individuals can navigate the vast flower patch of consumer choices with purpose and financial mindfulness.

Join me in the next chapter as we explore the hive's efficient communication system and draw parallels to effective financial communication within personal and professional spheres.

Mindful Spending: A Guided Approach to Financial Well-being

Mindful spending is a deliberate practice that involves spending money with conscious intention and alignment with personal values and goals. It also involves investing in learning and sometimes unlearning, as the world of personal finance is constantly evolving and changing. By staying updated and adaptable, individuals can make better financial decisions and achieve their desired outcomes. Here are ten meticulously crafted steps to guide you on your journey to becoming a mindful spender:

1. **Set Clear Financial Goals:**
   - Identify both short-term and long-term

financial objectives, whether it's saving for a dream vacation, purchasing a home, starting a business, or planning for retirement. Document your goals and revisit them regularly to stay focused. Make sure your goals are SMART: specific, measurable, achievable, relevant, and time-bound[1]

2. **Track Income and Expenses:**

  - Record your monthly earnings and expenditures using a spreadsheet, a dedicated app, or a journal. Categorize expenses into needs and wants, gaining insight into your spending patterns. Needs are essential expenses, such as rent, food, utilities, and insurance. Wants are discretionary expenses, such as entertainment, travel, and shopping[2]

3. **Craft a Comprehensive Budget:**

  - Based on your income and expenses, create a detailed plan for allocating funds each month. Assign specific amounts to categories such as housing, food, transportation, and entertainment. Allocate a portion for savings and investments aligned with your goals and risk tolerance. A popular budgeting method is the 50/30/20 rule, which suggests spending 50% of your income on needs, 30% on wants, and 20% on savings and investments[3]

4. **Regularly Review Your Budget:**

  - Compare your actual spending to the budget and make adjustments if necessary. Online tools and apps can aid in monitoring your budget and spending habits, ensuring you stay within your financial limits. Some of the best budgeting apps are Mint, YNAB, and Goodbudget[4]

5. **Evaluate Each Purchase:**

   ◦ Before making a purchase, ask critical questions: Do I truly need this? Will it bring me happiness? What is its longevity? Is there a better alternative? Consider the impact on your budget and goals. A useful technique is to calculate the cost per use or cost per hour of each purchase, which measures the value you get from it. For example, if you buy a $100 pair of shoes and wear them 100 times, the cost per use is $1. If you buy a $10 movie ticket and watch a 2-hour movie, the cost per hour is $5.

6. **Avoid Impulse Buying:**

   ◦ Guard against impulse buying by employing strategies such as waiting 24 hours before purchasing, adhering to a shopping list, avoiding shopping in emotional states, and unsubscribing from marketing emails and catalogs. Impulse buying is often triggered by psychological factors, such as stress, boredom, peer pressure, or social media. Impulse buying can lead to unnecessary or regrettable purchases, and waste your money.

7. **Prioritize Value Over Quantity:**

   ◦ Choose quality over quantity, aligning your spending with items that hold genuine value for you. Consider the benefits and costs of each spending decision, spending less on non-essential items and more on those that align with your values. Spend in a way that reflects your personal values, goals, and priorities. For example, you may value health and fitness, and spend more on organic food, gym membership, or sports equipment. You may value education and personal growth, and spend more on books, courses, or coaching.

8. **Invest in Experiences:**

- Research indicates that spending on experiences brings more happiness than material possessions. Experiences can enrich your life, create memories, and enhance your well-being. Spend money on experiences that align with your interests, passions, and values. For example, you may enjoy traveling and exploring new cultures, and spend money on flights, hotels, or tours. You may enjoy learning and acquiring new skills, and spend money on classes, workshops, or certifications.

  ○

9. **Save and Invest Wisely:**

- Prioritize saving for emergencies, retirement, and specific goals. Invest in a diversified portfolio, monitor its performance, and seek professional advice if needed. Educate yourself on various investment options, such as stocks, bonds, mutual funds, index funds, exchange-traded funds, options, real estate, and cryptocurrencies. Learn the basics of investing, such as risk-reward trade-off, asset allocation, diversification, and compounding.

10. **Practice Gratitude:**

- ◦ Cultivate gratitude for your income, expenses, and savings. Acknowledge the effort behind earning and managing your money. Appreciate the value money brings to your life, providing both happiness and security. Express thanks for the things and experiences that money can buy, and the opportunities and choices that money can provide.

Embark on this journey of mindful spending, where each financial decision is a conscious step toward achieving your goals and enhancing your overall well-being. Remember to invest in learning and sometimes unlearning, as the world of personal finance is constantly evolving and changing. By staying updated and adaptable, you can make better financial decisions and achieve your desired outcomes.

My Mindful and Memorable Trip to Vietnam and Thailand

I have always loved travelling, but sometimes it can be too expensive if you take the regular route like travel packages and stick to age-old systems of travelling. My friends returned from Vietnam with so many great stories that I too wanted to visit, but the cost they bore for the trip was extremely high. They had booked packages for most of the tour and stayed in luxurious hotels and resorts, and had maxed their credit cards. I decided to go for a solo trip, but on a budget. I did thorough research and made the following changes:

- Instead of hotels, I stayed in high-quality hostels that were rated high. I found them on websites like Hostelworld and Booking.com, and read the reviews and ratings. I chose hostels that were clean, safe, and well-located, and offered free breakfast, Wi-Fi, and other amenities. I paid an average of ₹500 per night, compared to ₹5000 or more for a hotel room.

- I used couch surfing and made friends forever. I joined the Couchsurfing website and app, and searched for hosts in Vietnam and Thailand who were willing to offer me a free couch or a spare room. I contacted them and introduced myself, and checked their references and profiles. I chose hosts who were friendly, hospitable, and had similar interests as me. I stayed with them for a few nights, and they showed me around their cities, shared their culture and cuisine, and gave me tips and recommendations. I had a wonderful time with them, and we became lifelong friends.

- I travelled with new friends and had a different experience. I met other solo travellers and backpackers in the hostels and couch surfing events, and we decided to travel together. We shared the costs of transportation, food, and activities, and had more fun and adventure. We rented scooters and bikes, and explored the countryside and the villages. We took local buses and trains, and experienced the authentic life of the people. We visited the famous attractions, such as the Cu Chi tunnels, the Halong Bay, and the Angkor Wat, and learned about the history and culture of the region.

- I did much more with a quarter of what they spent. I spent an average of ₹2000 per day, including accommodation, food, transportation, and activities. I stayed for 15 days in Vietnam and 2 days in Thailand, and spent a total of ₹51000, including the flights. My friends had spent over ₹200000 for their 10-day trip, and had missed out on many things that I had experienced. I felt proud and happy that I had managed to travel mindfully and save money, without compromising on quality or enjoyment.

- The bonus was that I came back to India via Thailand and stayed two extra days in Bangkok and did some shopping too. I found out that the flight from Ho Chi Minh City to Pune was almost twice as expensive as the flight from Bangkok to Pune. I decided to take advantage of this and booked a flight from Ho Chi Minh City to Bangkok, and then from Bangkok to Pune. I stayed for two nights in Bangkok, and explored the city and its attractions, such as the Grand Palace, the Wat Pho, and the Chatuchak market. I also did some shopping and bought some souvenirs and gifts for myself and my family.

I had an amazing trip to Vietnam and Thailand, and I learned a lot from it. I learned how to travel mindfully and spend wisely, and how to make the most of every opportunity and experience. I learned how to meet new people and make friends, and how to appreciate different cultures and lifestyles. I learned how to be grateful and happy, and how to live in the present. I came back with a lot of memories and stories, and a lot of wisdom and joy.

CHAPTER 7:

"Navigating Economic Seasons: Adapting Like A Hive"

I n the intricate ballet of nature, honey bees showcase an extraordinary ability to adapt seamlessly to the changing seasons. As we delve into the hive's collective wisdom, we unravel invaluable insights on how individuals can navigate economic uncertainties with resilience and adaptability.

The Hive's Seasonal Symphony

Honey bees, attuned to the rhythms of nature, adeptly adjust their activities in response to the shifting seasons. From the vibrancy of spring to the abundance of summer and the austerity of winter, each season dictates specific hive behaviors. The bees instinctively reallocate their focus, resources, and strategies to thrive despite the unpredictable nature of the external environment.

For example, in spring, when flowers are abundant and nectar is flowing, the bees are busy collecting pollen and making honey. They also increase their population by producing more brood (baby bees). In summer, when the temperature is high and the hive is crowded, the bees maintain their honey production and ventilation. They also swarm (split into two groups) to find new homes. In fall, when the flowers are scarce and the nectar is drying up, the bees reduce their population and store their honey for winter. They also defend their hive from predators and parasites. In winter, when the temperature is low and the food is limited, the bees cluster together to keep warm and feed on their honey. They also reduce their activity and metabolism to conserve energy.

Economic Seasons in Human Life

Much like the natural world, human economic landscapes experience seasons of growth, stability, and recession. Understanding the parallels between the hive's seasonal adaptations and economic fluctuations equips individuals with the foresight to make informed financial decisions.

According to the National Bureau of Economic Research (NBER), the average economic cycle in the U.S. has lasted roughly five and a half years since 1950, although these cycles can vary in length[1]. Factors to indicate the stages include gross domestic product, consumer spending, interest rates, and inflation.

For example, in a growth phase, when the economy is expanding and the income is rising, individuals can increase their spending and saving. They can also invest in opportunities and take calculated risks. In a stability phase, when the economy is steady and the income is stable, individuals can maintain their spending and saving. They can also diversify their income and investments and prepare for future changes. In a recession phase, when the economy is contracting and the income is falling, individuals can reduce their spending and debt. They can also prioritize their needs and goals and seek alternative sources of income and support.

Lessons from the Hive:

1. Preparation for Winter:
- Honey bees diligently prepare for the harshness of winter by stockpiling honey during the abundance of summer and fall. Individuals can adopt a similar approach, building financial reserves during prosperous times to weather economic downturns.
- According to a survey by Bankrate, only 39% of Americans have enough savings to cover a $1,000 emergency[2]. This means that many people are living paycheck to paycheck and are vulnerable to unexpected expenses or income shocks. To avoid this situation, individuals should aim to save at least three to six months' worth of living expenses in an emergency fund. This will provide a cushion in case of job loss, medical bills, or other unforeseen events.

2. Diversification of Resources:
- Bees diversify their foraging efforts, recognizing that different flowers bloom in different seasons. Likewise, individuals can diversify their income streams and investments to mitigate the impact of economic uncertainties.
- According to a report by the Pew Research Center, the median household income in the U.S. declined

by 9% from 1999 to 2014, after adjusting for inflation[3]. This means that many people are earning less than they used to and are struggling to keep up with the rising cost of living. To cope with this situation, individuals should seek to create multiple sources of income, such as side hustles, freelancing, or passive income. This will increase their cash flow and reduce their dependence on a single employer.

- According to a study by Vanguard, the average annual return of the U.S. stock market from 1926 to 2019 was 10.1%, but it varied widely from year to year, ranging from -43.1% in 1931 to 54.2% in 1933[4]. This means that investing in the stock market can be rewarding but also risky and volatile. To reduce this risk, individuals should diversify their investments across different asset classes, such as stocks, bonds, real estate, and commodities. This will balance their portfolio and smooth out their returns.

3. Efficient Resource Allocation:

- The hive allocates resources with precision, directing efforts towards critical needs during lean times. In economic downturns, individuals can streamline expenses, focusing on essentials and reallocating resources strategically.
- According to a report by the Bureau of Labor Statistics, the average annual expenditure per consumer unit in the U.S. in 2019 was $63,036, of which $20,679 (32.8%) was spent on housing, $10,742 (17%) on transportation, and $8,169 (13%) on food[5]. This means that many people are spending a large portion of their income on basic

necessities and have little room for discretionary spending. To optimize their expenses, individuals should review their spending habits and identify areas where they can cut costs or find cheaper alternatives. For example, they can refinance their mortgage, switch to public transportation, or cook at home more often.

4. Collaborative Adaptation:
- Bees work collaboratively to ensure the survival of the hive. Similarly, individuals can leverage community support, seek professional advice, and engage in collaborative efforts to navigate economic challenges.
- According to a survey by the Federal Reserve, 37% of U.S. adults would not be able to pay for an unexpected $400 expense with cash, savings, or a credit card that they could pay off in full, and 12% would not be able to pay for it at all. This means that many people are financially vulnerable and isolated and have limited options to cope with economic shocks. To overcome this situation, individuals should seek help from their family, friends, or community, such as borrowing money, sharing resources, or joining a support group. They should also consult with financial experts, such as advisors, counselors, or coaches, who can offer guidance, education, or solutions.

5. Resilience through Adaptability:
- Honey bees showcase resilience by adapting their behaviors to the demands of each season. Individuals can cultivate financial resilience by embracing adaptability, learning new skills, and

exploring alternative avenues during economic shifts.

- According to a report by the World Economic Forum, 42% of the core skills required for most jobs are expected to change by 2022, and 54% of all employees will need significant reskilling and upskilling by 2022. This means that the labor market is undergoing rapid and profound changes and that many workers will need to adapt to new technologies, industries, and roles. To prepare for this change, individuals should invest in their human capital, such as learning new skills, acquiring new credentials, or pursuing new careers. They should also be open to new opportunities, such as starting a business, joining a startup, or working remotely.

Economic Forecasting: Insights from the Hive

The hive's ability to adapt offers valuable lessons for economic forecasting in personal finance. By closely observing economic indicators, understanding market trends, and staying informed, individuals can anticipate and prepare for economic shifts.

Some of the key economic indicators that can help individuals forecast the economic seasons are:

- Gross Domestic Product (GDP): This is the total value of goods and services produced in a country in a given period. It measures the size and growth of the economy. A positive GDP growth indicates an expansion, while a negative GDP growth indicates a contraction. A recession is typically defined as two consecutive quarters of negative GDP growth.

- Consumer Price Index (CPI): This is a measure of the average change in prices paid by consumers for a basket of goods and services over time. It measures the level and rate of inflation. A moderate inflation indicates a healthy economy, while a high inflation or a deflation indicates an unhealthy economy.

- Unemployment Rate: This is the percentage of the labor force that is unemployed and actively looking for work. It measures the level and trend of unemployment. A low unemployment rate indicates a strong labor market, while a high unemployment rate indicates a weak labor market.

- Consumer Confidence Index (CCI): This is a measure of consumers' optimism or pessimism about the current and future state of the economy. It measures the level and direction of consumer sentiment. A high consumer confidence indicates a positive outlook, while a low consumer confidence indicates a negative outlook.

Cultivating Financial Flexibility

In the face of economic uncertainty, flexibility becomes a crucial asset. Learning from the hive's adaptability, individuals can proactively adjust their financial strategies, explore new opportunities, and remain agile in the ever-changing economic landscape.

Some of the ways that individuals can cultivate financial flexibility are:

- Build an emergency fund: This is a savings account that can cover three to six months' worth of living expenses in case of an emergency, such as job loss, medical bills, or car repairs. It provides a safety net and a peace of mind. According to a survey by Bankrate, only 39% of Americans have enough savings to cover a $1,000 emergency1. To avoid this situation, individuals should aim to save at least 10% of their income each month and keep their emergency fund in a high-yield savings account or a liquid mutual fund.
- Pay off debt: This is the process of reducing or

eliminating the amount of money owed to creditors, such as credit cards, student loans, or mortgages. It frees up cash flow and reduces interest payments. According to a report by the Federal Reserve, the total household debt in the U.S. reached $14.64 trillion in the first quarter of 2021, of which $820 billion was credit card debt2. To cope with this situation, individuals should follow the debt snowball or debt avalanche method, pay more than the minimum payment, and negotiate lower interest rates or settlement offers with their creditors.

- Use credit cards wisely: This is the process of using credit cards as a tool to earn rewards, build credit, and access exclusive offers, without falling into debt or paying unnecessary fees. According to a report by Experian, the average credit card limit in the U.S. was $22,589 in 2020, but the average credit card balance was only $5,3133. This means that many people are not using their credit cards to their full potential or are using them irresponsibly. To optimize their credit card usage, individuals should follow these tips:

- Use credit cards only when they have or will have money to pay off the balance in full each month. This will avoid interest charges and late fees, and improve their credit score. According to a study by CreditCards.com, the average credit card interest rate in the U.S. was 16.15% in 20204. This means that carrying a balance can cost a lot of money in the long run. For example, if someone has a $1,000 balance on a credit card with a 16.15% interest rate, and they pay only the minimum payment of $25 each month, it will take them 56 months to pay off the balance and they will pay $435 in interest.

- Choose credit cards that suit their spending patterns, goals, and preferences. There are many types of credit cards available, such as cashback, rewards, travel, balance transfer, low interest, secured, and student cards. Each card has its own benefits, features, fees, and eligibility criteria. Individuals should compare different cards and select the ones that offer the most value for their needs. For example, if someone travels frequently, they may benefit from a travel card that offers miles, lounge access, and travel insurance. If someone wants to save money, they may benefit from a cashback card that offers a percentage of their spending back as cash or statement credit.

- Keep an eye on their credit card utilization, which is the ratio of their credit card balance to their credit card limit. This is one of the most important factors that affect their credit score. According to FICO, the optimal credit card utilization is below 30%5. This means that individuals should try to keep their balance below 30% of their limit on each card and across all cards. For example, if someone has a credit card with a $10,000 limit and a $3,000 balance, their credit card utilization is 30%. If they have two credit cards, one with a $10,000 limit and a $3,000 balance, and another with a $5,000 limit and a $1,000 balance, their credit card utilization is 28.6% ($4,000/$14,000). To lower their credit card utilization, individuals should pay off their balance as soon as possible, request a higher credit limit, or use multiple cards for different purchases.

- Be aware of the hidden charges and fees that may apply to their credit cards, such as annual fees, foreign transaction fees, cash advance fees, late payment fees, overlimit fees, and returned payment fees. These fees can add up quickly and eat into their rewards and savings. Individuals should read the fine print of their credit card agreements and statements, and avoid actions that may trigger these fees. For example, if someone has a credit card that charges a 3% foreign transaction fee, they should avoid using it for purchases in other currencies. If someone has a credit card that charges a $35 late payment fee, they should set up automatic payments or reminders to pay their bill on time.

· Use credit cards only with trusted merchants and websites, and protect their credit card information from fraud and identity theft. According to a report by Javelin Strategy & Research, 14.4 million Americans were victims of identity fraud in 2019, and 23% of them had their credit card information stolen. To prevent this situation, individuals should use secure and encrypted websites, avoid phishing emails and calls, monitor their credit card statements and credit reports, and report any suspicious or unauthorized transactions to their credit card issuer. They should also use features such as virtual card numbers, biometric authentication, and alerts to enhance their credit card security.

· Avoid cash withdrawals from their credit cards, unless it is absolutely necessary. Cash withdrawals from credit cards are considered as cash advances, which are subject to high interest rates, fees, and limits. Unlike regular purchases, cash advances do not have a grace period, which means that interest starts accruing from the day of the withdrawal. According to a survey by CreditCards.com, the average cash advance interest rate in the U.S. was 24.8% in 2020, and the average cash advance fee was 5% or $10, whichever is higher. This means that withdrawing cash from a credit card can be very expensive and should be avoided as much as possible. For example, if someone withdraws $500 from a credit card with a 24.8% interest rate and a 5% fee, they will pay $25 as a fee and $10.27 as interest in the first month, assuming they pay off the balance in full.

- I have more than 10 credit cards and I use them based on the benefits they have to offer. I use credit cards when I know I have or I will have money to pay off the card, entitling me to various benefits like points, cashback, discounts, and offers. However, many people use credit cards when they don't have money to spend, which can lead to debt and financial stress. Credit cards are a great tool for free EMI conversion, when you don't have cash in hand to pay or ATM is too far away, when there are exclusive credit card offers, etc. But they should be used wisely and responsibly, following the tips mentioned above.

CHAPTER 8:

"The Hive-Mind Approach To Financial Planning"

I n the heart of the hive, a mesmerizing phenomenon unfolds —the hive mind. A collective consciousness that guides the hive's decisions, ensuring its prosperity and survival. As we delve into this intricate web of communication and collaboration, we unravel the transformative potential of adopting a hive-mind approach to financial planning.

The Hive's Collective Wisdom

Within the hive, decisions are not made in isolation. Instead, the collective wisdom of the colony shapes choices that impact the entire community. The bees communicate through intricate dances, pheromones, and signals, fostering a unified understanding that guides their actions. This collaborative decision-making process ensures the hive's success in the face of challenges and opportunities.

According to a study by Thomas Seeley and colleagues, honeybees can make optimal decisions about their nest sites by using a decentralized system of information sharing and collective assessment1. The study found that the bees can achieve a 99% success rate in choosing the best among several options, even when individual bees have limited information and cognitive abilities. The key to their success is the use of positive feedback (waggle dances) and negative feedback (stop signals) to reach a consensus among the group.

The Power of Collective Financial Planning

Drawing parallels from the hive, individuals can harness the strength of collective decision-making in their financial planning endeavors. Embracing a hive-mind approach involves recognizing the value of diverse perspectives, seeking advice, and engaging in open communication about financial goals and strategies.

According to a survey by Charles Schwab, 75% of Americans who have a written financial plan say they feel financially stable, compared to 34% of those who don't have a plan2. The survey also found that those who have a plan are more likely to have a positive outlook on their finances, save more, invest more, and pay off debt faster. However, only 25% of Americans actually have a written financial plan, and 45% of those who don't have one say they don't know how to create one.

One way to overcome this challenge is to seek the help of a financial planner, a professional who can provide guidance, education, and solutions for various financial goals and needs. According to a study by Vanguard, working with a financial planner can add about 3% in net returns to a portfolio over time, through a combination of asset allocation, cost-effective implementation, rebalancing, behavioral coaching, and tax-efficient strategies3.

Another way to benefit from collective financial planning is to join or create a financial community, a network of individuals with shared financial interests and goals. This community can provide emotional support, share valuable insights, and serve as a source of inspiration and accountability. According to a study by Northwestern Mutual, 70% of Americans say they feel happier and more confident when they talk about their finances with others, and 44% say they have improved their financial situation by doing so.

The benefits of collective financial planning are not limited to the United States. In fact, other regions, such as India, China, and Europe, have their own data and statistics that show the value of adopting a hive-mind approach to financial planning.

In India, according to a report by the National Council of Applied Economic Research, only 33% of households have a financial plan, and only 24% of households consult a financial advisor. The report also found that 62% of households rely on informal sources of borrowing, such as moneylenders, relatives, and friends, and only 10% of households have any form of insurance. The report suggests that there is a huge gap in financial literacy and inclusion in India, which hinders the financial well-being of millions of people.

One way to bridge this gap is to leverage the power of digital platforms and social networks, which can enable greater access to financial information, advice, and services. According to a report by the Boston Consulting Group, India has the second-largest internet user base in the world, with 560 million users, and the largest social media user base, with 310 million users. The report also found that 40% of internet users in India use digital platforms for financial transactions, and 20% of internet users in India use social media for financial advice. The report suggests that digital and social platforms can create a more inclusive and collaborative financial ecosystem in India, where individuals can learn from each other, share best practices, and access affordable and convenient financial solutions.

In China, according to a report by the China Banking Association and PwC, 72% of households have a financial plan, and 58% of households consult a financial advisor. The report also found that 74% of households use online platforms for financial transactions, and 66% of households use online platforms for financial information. The report suggests that China has a high level of financial awareness and digital adoption, which creates a favorable environment for collective financial planning.

One way to enhance this environment is to foster a culture of trust and transparency, which can encourage more open and honest communication about financial matters. According to a survey by Edelman, China has the highest level of trust in financial institutions among 28 countries, with 88% of respondents expressing trust. However, the survey also found that China has the lowest level of trust in financial information from the media, with only 36% of respondents expressing trust. The survey suggests that there is a need for more reliable and independent sources of financial information and advice in China, which can help individuals make more informed and confident financial decisions.

In Europe, according to a report by ING, 52% of households have a financial plan, and 42% of households consult a financial advisor. The report also found that 56% of households use online platforms for financial transactions, and 48% of households use online platforms for financial information. The report suggests that Europe has a moderate level of financial planning and digital usage, which varies across different countries and regions.

One way to improve this situation is to leverage the potential of open data, which can enable easier and safer financial data sharing. According to a report by the McKinsey Global Institute, the boost to the economy from broad adoption of open-data ecosystems could range from about 1 to 1.5 percent of GDP in 2030 in the European Union and the United Kingdom. The report also notes that open data can create value for all market participants, such as individuals, financial institutions, and regulators, by enabling more accurate credit risk evaluation, improved product delivery, and stronger fraud protection.

Lessons from the Hive:

1. Diversity in Decision-Makers:

- The hive thrives on the diversity of worker bees, each contributing unique skills and perspectives. In financial planning, diverse input—from financial advisors, family members, and professionals—can lead to well-rounded decisions that consider various angles.

- According to a report by McKinsey, companies with more diverse executive teams are 33% more likely to outperform their peers on profitability, and companies with more diverse boards are 43% more likely to do so. The report suggests that diversity brings a variety of experiences, perspectives, and insights that can enhance decision-making, innovation, and customer satisfaction.

- Similarly, individuals can benefit from seeking diverse input in their financial planning, as different sources of advice can offer different types of value. For example, a financial advisor can provide expert knowledge, a family member can provide emotional support, and a professional can provide industry-specific insights. By combining these inputs, individuals can make more informed and balanced financial decisions.

- The importance of diversity in decision-making is not limited to the corporate world. In fact, other regions, such as India, China, and Europe, have their own data and statistics that show the value of seeking diverse input in financial planning.

- In India, according to a report by the National Council of Applied Economic Research, only 33% of households have a financial plan, and only 24% of households consult a financial advisor. The report also found that 62% of households rely on informal sources of borrowing, such as moneylenders, relatives, and friends, and only 10% of households have any form of insurance. The report suggests that there is a huge gap in financial literacy and inclusion in India, which hinders the financial well-being of millions of people.

- One way to bridge this gap is to seek the help of a financial planner, a professional who can provide guidance, education, and solutions for various financial goals and needs. According to a report by the Financial Planning Standards Board India, there are only about 3,000 certified financial planners in India, serving a population of 1.3 billion people. The report suggests that there is a need for more qualified and competent financial planners in India, who can help individuals make better financial decisions.

- Another way to benefit from diverse input in financial planning is to consult with family members, especially elders, who may have more experience and wisdom in managing money. According to a survey by HSBC, 69% of Indians say they have learned the most about money from their parents, compared to 54% of the global average. The survey also found that 77% of Indians say they regularly discuss money matters with their family, compared to 61% of the global average. The survey suggests that Indians value the role of family in their financial planning, and can learn from their insights and advice.

- In China, according to a report by the China Banking Association and PwC, 72% of households have a financial plan, and 58% of households consult a financial advisor. The report also found that 74% of households use online platforms for financial transactions, and 66% of households use online platforms for financial information. The report suggests that China has a high level of financial awareness and digital adoption, which creates a favorable environment for seeking diverse input in financial planning.

- One way to leverage this environment is to use online platforms and forums that connect people with similar financial goals, challenges, or interests. For example, Zhihu is a popular question-and-answer website in China, where users can ask and answer questions on various topics, including personal finance. According to its website, Zhihu has over 220 million registered users and over 34 million questions and answers on personal finance. These platforms and forums allow users to exchange information, opinions, and experiences, and learn from each other.

- Another way to benefit from diverse input in financial planning is to consult with professionals from different fields and industries, who may have specialized knowledge and insights. According to a report by the China Institute of Certified Financial Planners, there are over 170,000 certified financial planners in China, serving a population of 1.4 billion people. The report also notes that certified financial planners in China come from various backgrounds, such as banking, insurance, securities, accounting, and law. The report suggests that there is a diverse pool of financial experts in China, who can offer valuable advice and solutions to individuals.

- In Europe, according to a report by ING, 52% of households have a financial plan, and 42% of households consult a financial advisor. The report also found that 56% of households use online platforms for financial transactions, and 48% of households use online platforms for financial information. The report suggests that Europe has a moderate level of financial planning and digital usage, which varies across different countries and regions.

- One way to improve this situation is to seek the help of a financial planner, a professional who can provide guidance, education, and solutions for various financial goals and needs. According to a report by the Financial Planning Standards Board, there are over 170,000 certified financial planners in Europe, serving a population of 741 million people. The report also notes that certified financial planners in Europe adhere to high standards of ethics, competence, and professionalism. The report suggests that there is a need for more awareness and recognition of the value of financial planning and financial planners in Europe, who can help individuals make better financial decisions.

- Another way to benefit from diverse input in financial planning is to consult with peers and friends, who may have similar financial situations and goals. According to a survey by ING, 44% of Europeans say they discuss money matters with their friends, and 35% of Europeans say they have learned the most about money from their friends. The survey also found that 51% of Europeans say they would trust their friends' advice on money matters, and 41% of Europeans say they would be willing to share their financial data with their friends. The survey suggests that Europeans value the role of friends in their financial planning, and can learn from their insights and advice.

I can help you create a simple financial planner that can guide you to achieve your financial goals. Here are the steps to follow:

1. Set your financial goals. Think about what you want to accomplish with your money, both in the short term and the long term. For example, you may want to save for an emergency fund, pay off debt, buy a house, or retire comfortably. Write down your goals and prioritize them according to their importance and urgency.

2. Assess your current financial situation. Review your

income, expenses, assets, and liabilities. Calculate your net worth, which is the difference between your assets and liabilities. Calculate your cash flow, which is the difference between your income and expenses. Identify your strengths and weaknesses, and look for areas where you can improve your financial health.

3. Create a budget. A budget is a plan for how you will spend and save your money each month. It helps you to live within your means, allocate your money to your goals, and track your progress. To create a budget, list all your income sources and fixed and variable expenses. Subtract your expenses from your income to get your surplus or deficit. If you have a surplus, decide how much you will save and invest for your goals. If you have a deficit, look for ways to increase your income or reduce your expenses.

4. Build an emergency fund. An emergency fund is a savings account that can cover three to six months' worth of living expenses in case of an unexpected event, such as job loss, medical bills, or car repairs. It provides a safety net and a peace of mind. To build an emergency fund, set a target amount based on your monthly expenses, and save a portion of your income each month until you reach your goal. Keep your emergency fund in a high-yield savings account or a liquid mutual fund that is easily accessible and earns interest.

5. Pay off debt. Debt is money that you owe to others, such as credit cards, student loans, or mortgages. It can reduce your cash flow, limit your financial options, and affect your credit score. To pay off debt, list all your debts and their interest rates, balances, and minimum payments. Choose a debt repayment strategy, such as the debt snowball or debt avalanche method, and pay more than the minimum payment

each month. Avoid taking on new debt or using credit cards until you are debt-free.

6. Save and invest for your goals. Saving and investing are ways to grow your money over time and achieve your financial goals. Saving is putting money aside in a safe and liquid account, such as a savings account or a certificate of deposit. Investing is putting money into assets that have the potential to increase in value, such as stocks, bonds, mutual funds, or real estate. To save and invest for your goals, decide how much you need, how long you have, and how much risk you are willing to take. Choose the appropriate saving or investing vehicles for your goals, and contribute a percentage of your income regularly. Monitor your performance and adjust your strategy as needed.

7. Plan for retirement. Retirement is the stage of life when you stop working and live on your savings and investments. To plan for retirement, estimate how much income you will need, how long you will live, and what sources of income you will have, such as social security, pensions, or annuities. Calculate how much you need to save and invest for retirement, and choose the suitable retirement accounts, such as 401(k), IRA, or Roth IRA. Maximize your contributions and take advantage of employer matching, tax benefits, and compounding interest. Review your plan periodically and make changes as your situation changes.

These are the basic steps to create a simple financial planner. However, you may also want to consider other aspects of financial planning, such as insurance, estate planning, tax planning, and education planning. You can also consult a professional financial planner, who can provide you with more personalized and comprehensive advice and solutions.

CHAPTER 9:

"Honey Bee Wisdom In Real Life: Case Studies Of Financial Success"

I n the real-world hive of personal finance, individuals have drawn inspiration from the wisdom of honey bees, implementing strategies that mirror the precision and purpose seen in the buzzing microcosm. As we delve into the hive of human financial experiences, let's explore case studies that highlight the tangible successes achieved by those who embraced honey bee-inspired financial practices.

Case Study 1: The Nectar of Strategic Savings Meet Raj and Nisha, a couple in their early thirties with dreams of homeownership and a secure future.

Challenge: Limited income and high aspirations.

Raj and Nisha are both software engineers working for a multinational company in Bangalore, India. They earn a combined monthly income of 150,000 rupees (about $2,000), which is above the average income in India, but not enough to afford a comfortable lifestyle in the city. They have to pay rent, utilities, transportation, food, and other expenses, leaving them with little savings at the end of the month. They also have to support their parents, who live in a rural village and depend on their remittances.

Raj and Nisha have always dreamed of buying their own home, where they can start a family and enjoy more space and privacy. They also want to save for their retirement, their children's education, and their parents' health care. However, they are daunted by the high cost of living and the low returns on traditional savings instruments, such as bank deposits and government bonds. They wonder how they can achieve their financial goals with their limited income and resources.

Honey Bee-Inspired Strategy:

Raj and Nisha adopted the honey bee's approach to strategic saving. They meticulously assessed their financial landscape, identifying various "flowers" of opportunity. Allocating specific portions of their income to different financial goals, they created a diversified financial garden.

They started by creating a budget, tracking their income and expenses, and identifying areas where they could save more and spend less. They used online tools and apps, such as Money Manager and Walnut, to help them monitor and manage their finances. They also set up automatic transfers from their salary accounts to their savings accounts, ensuring that they saved before they spent.

They then divided their savings into three categories: short-term, medium-term, and long-term. For their short-term savings, they aimed to build an emergency fund that could cover six months' worth of living expenses, in case of any unforeseen events, such as job loss, medical bills, or car repairs. They kept their emergency fund in a high-interest savings account, which offered them liquidity and security.

For their medium-term savings, they aimed to save for a down payment on a home, which they planned to buy in five years.

They estimated that they would need at least 20% of the property value as a down payment, which meant they had to save about 1.2 million rupees (about $16,000) for a modest two-bedroom apartment in the outskirts of the city. They invested their medium-term savings in a balanced mutual fund, which offered them a mix of equity and debt, and a higher return than a savings account.

For their long-term savings, they aimed to save for their retirement, their children's education, and their parents' health care, which they expected to need in 20 years or more. They estimated that they would need at least 10 million rupees (about $133,000) to maintain their current standard of living in retirement, assuming an inflation rate of 5% and a life expectancy of 80 years. They also estimated that they would need at least 5 million rupees (about $67,000) to fund their children's higher education, assuming they would have two children and send them to a reputable university. They also set aside some money for their parents' health care, in case they needed any medical treatment or assistance in their old age. They invested their long-term savings in an aggressive mutual fund, which offered them a higher exposure to equity and a higher potential return over time.

Outcome:

Over the years, Raj and Nisha managed to save for a down payment on a home, build an emergency fund, and invest for long-term goals. Their disciplined approach allowed them to weather unexpected financial challenges, and their financial garden flourished.

They were able to buy their dream home in 2026, after saving enough for a down payment and securing a home loan at a favorable interest rate. They moved into their new apartment, which was spacious, comfortable, and located in a good neighborhood. They were delighted to have their own place, where they could raise their children and host their parents and friends.

They also maintained their emergency fund, which came in handy when they faced some financial difficulties, such as a temporary salary cut due to the COVID-19 pandemic, a car accident that damaged their vehicle, and a surgery that their father had to undergo. They were able to cope with these situations without having to borrow money or dip into their other savings.

They also continued to invest for their long-term goals, which grew steadily over time. They benefited from the power of compounding, which increased their returns exponentially. They also diversified their investments, spreading their risk across different asset classes, sectors, and markets. They also rebalanced their portfolio periodically, adjusting their asset allocation according to their changing risk appetite and time horizon.

By 2046, Raj and Nisha had accumulated enough wealth to retire comfortably, fund their children's education, and support their parents' health care. They were able to enjoy their golden years, traveling the world, pursuing their hobbies, and spending time with their family and friends. They were also able to leave a legacy for their children and grandchildren, passing on their financial wisdom and values.

Case Study 2: Collaborative Investing Introducing the Patel family—three generations navigating the complexities of modern finance.

Challenge: Balancing financial priorities and preserving wealth for future generations.

The Patel family is a typical Indian joint family, consisting of three generations living under one roof. The patriarch of the family is Ramesh, a 65-year-old retired businessman, who started a successful textile company in the 1980s. He is married to Sunita, a 60-year-old homemaker, who takes care of the household chores and the family's finances. They have two sons, Amit and Rohit, who are both in their thirties and work in the family business. Amit is married to Priya, a 32-year-old software engineer, who works for a multinational company. They have a 5-year-old daughter, Aisha, who goes to a private school. Rohit is married to Neha, a 30-year-old doctor, who works in a government hospital. They have a 3-year-old son, Arjun, who goes to a daycare center.

The Patel family has a substantial amount of wealth, which they have accumulated over the years through their business and investments. They own a large house in a posh area of Mumbai, several properties across India, and a diversified portfolio of stocks, bonds, mutual funds, gold, and cryptocurrencies. They also have a generous amount of cash in their bank accounts, which they use for their daily expenses and emergencies.

The Patel family has different financial priorities and preferences, which sometimes create conflicts and disagreements. Ramesh and Sunita are conservative and risk-averse, preferring to invest in safe and stable assets, such as fixed deposits, government bonds, and gold. They also like to save a large portion of their income, and spend only on essential items. They are concerned about the future of their family business, and want to ensure that it remains profitable and competitive. They also want to preserve their wealth for their grandchildren, and pass on their values and traditions to them.

Amit and Rohit are more aggressive and risk-tolerant, preferring to invest in high-growth and high-return assets, such as stocks, mutual funds, and cryptocurrencies. They also like to spend a large portion of their income, and enjoy a lavish lifestyle. They are interested in expanding their family business, and exploring new opportunities and markets. They also want to achieve financial independence, and pursue their own passions and interests.

Priya and Neha are more balanced and moderate, preferring to invest in a mix of assets, such as stocks, bonds, mutual funds, and gold. They also like to save and spend a reasonable portion of their income, and maintain a comfortable lifestyle. They are supportive of their husbands' ambitions, but also have their own career goals and aspirations. They also want to provide the best education and opportunities for their children, and encourage them to follow their dreams.

Aisha and Arjun are too young to have any financial priorities or preferences, but they are exposed to different influences and expectations from their parents and grandparents. They are curious and eager to learn about money and finance, and often ask questions and observe their elders' behaviors.

Honey Bee-Inspired Strategy:

The Patel family embraced the hive-mind approach to financial planning. Different generations collaborated, bringing diverse perspectives to the table. They pooled resources for investments, considering the long-term prosperity of the entire family.

They started by having regular and open conversations about their financial goals, needs, and challenges. They used online tools and apps, such as Moneycontrol and ETMoney, to help them track and manage their finances. They also consulted a professional financial planner, who helped them create a comprehensive financial plan that aligned with their family's vision and values.

They then divided their investments into three categories: family, individual, and legacy. For their family investments, they aimed to grow and protect their family's wealth, and support their family's business and expenses. They invested a large portion of their wealth in a diversified portfolio of assets, such as stocks, bonds, mutual funds, real estate, and gold. They followed a balanced asset allocation strategy, which suited their risk appetite and time horizon. They also rebalanced their portfolio periodically, to maintain their desired asset mix and optimize their returns.

For their individual investments, they aimed to achieve their personal financial goals, such as buying a car, traveling abroad, or starting a new venture. They invested a smaller portion of their wealth in a customized portfolio of assets, which matched their individual risk profiles and preferences. They followed a goal-based investing strategy, which linked their investments to specific goals and milestones. They also monitored their progress regularly, and made adjustments as needed.

For their legacy investments, they aimed to preserve and pass on their wealth to their children and grandchildren, and support their social and philanthropic causes. They invested a minimal portion of their wealth in a conservative portfolio of assets, such as fixed deposits, government securities, and insurance policies. They followed a legacy planning strategy, which involved creating a will, a trust, and a succession plan for their family business. They also donated some of their wealth to various charities and foundations, which aligned with their values and principles.

Outcome:

By adopting the hive-mind approach to financial planning, the Patel family achieved financial harmony and success. Their collaborative and diversified investment strategy enabled them to balance their family, individual, and legacy goals, and create a lasting financial legacy for their future generations.

- Another example of hive mind can be seen in Wikipedia, which is an online encyclopedia that anyone can edit and contribute to. Wikipedia relies on the collective wisdom and knowledge of millions of volunteers, who collaborate and coordinate to create and improve articles on various topics2.
- A third example of hive mind can be observed in social media, which is a platform that connects people with similar interests, opinions, and goals. Social media users can share information, opinions, and experiences, and influence each other's behaviors and attitudes. Social media can also create a sense of community and belonging among users, who may feel more confident and happier when they interact with others3.

CHAPTER 10:

Sustaining Financial Ecosystems:

Leaving a Legacy Like Honey Bees

I n the final chapter of our financial hive exploration, we explore the profound concept of leaving a lasting legacy—a legacy that reflects the sustained impact honey bees have on their natural ecosystems. Just as the honey bee's role in nurturing and preserving its environment benefits countless species, individuals can cultivate a financial legacy that transcends their lifetime, creating a positive ripple effect for generations to come.

The Bee's Enduring Impact: Honey bees are more than just nectar collectors; they are vital pollinators, enabling the growth of plants and ensuring the health of ecosystems. Their diligent efforts contribute to the richness and diversity of life. According to a report by the United Nations Environment Programme (UNEP), bees pollinate food crops that provide around 90% of the world's food, which demonstrates how important their role is in the natural ecosystem1. Similarly, individuals can aspire to create a financial legacy that goes beyond personal wealth, enhancing the lives of their families and communities.

Principles of a Lasting Financial Legacy:

1. **Strategic Planning for Generations:** Just as honey bees plan for the long-term survival of their colonies, individuals can adopt a long-term perspective in their financial planning. Strategic investment, prudent estate planning, and the transfer of financial wisdom can ensure that the benefits of financial acumen extend to future generations. According to a study, only 44% of Americans have a will, which means many people are not prepared for the distribution of their assets after their death2. A well-planned estate plan can help avoid conflicts, taxes, and legal fees, and ensure that the financial legacy is passed on according to the individual's wishes.

2. **Collaborative Prosperity:** The collaborative spirit within a hive serves as a powerful metaphor for family and community collaboration in financial matters. Families that actively engage in open discussions about money, investments, and long-term goals are better positioned to build a collective prosperity that endures. According to a survey, 70% of wealthy families lose their wealth by the second generation, and 90% by the third, due to lack of communication and trust among family members3. By fostering a culture of financial transparency and cooperation, families can avoid conflicts, align their values, and support each other's financial goals.

3. **Environmental Stewardship:** Honey bees are integral to the health of ecosystems, and individuals can contribute to the health of their financial ecosystems. Sustainable and ethical investing, along with responsible consumption, aligns with the principles of environmental stewardship, leaving behind a legacy of mindful financial choices. According to

a report, sustainable investing assets reached $35.3 trillion in 2020, representing 36% of all professionally managed assets across five major markets4. By investing in companies that have a positive social and environmental impact, individuals can align their financial legacy with their values and support the causes they care about.

4. **Financial Education and Empowerment:** Honey bees communicate vital information through intricate dances. Similarly, passing on financial knowledge becomes a dance of empowerment. Educating family members, especially the younger generation, equips them with the skills to make informed financial decisions, ensuring the legacy of financial literacy. According to a study, only 57% of adults in the world are financially literate, and the gap is even wider among women, the poor, and lower-educated people5. By providing financial education and empowerment, individuals can help their family and community members achieve financial independence, security, and well-being.

The Ripple Effect of Financial Abundance: As honey bees create a ripple effect through the pollination of flowers, individuals can leave a positive financial ripple effect that reaches far beyond their immediate sphere. A legacy built on principles of sustainability, collaboration, and empowerment serves as a testament to the lasting impact of thoughtful financial stewardship.

Building a Financial Community and Strategic Investments

In the journey to build a lasting legacy, consider the profound impact of building a financial community and implementing strategic investments. Much like honey bees collaborating to achieve collective success, our financial strategies can benefit from a cooperative mindset.

Making Friends with Like-Minded Individuals: In the pursuit of leaving a legacy, the strength of community can be as crucial as individual efforts. Surround yourself with individuals who share similar financial aspirations. Creating a community of like-minded people fosters an environment where ideas, experiences, and strategies can be shared. The synergy of engaging with individuals who align with your financial values not only provides valuable insights but also offers a support system on the path to financial success. For example, you can join online forums, social media groups, or clubs that focus on financial topics that interest you, such as investing, saving, budgeting, or entrepreneurship. You can also attend workshops, seminars, or webinars that feature experts or peers who can share their financial knowledge and experiences. By connecting with people who have similar financial goals and challenges, you can learn from each other, exchange tips and advice, and motivate each other to achieve your financial objectives.

Smart Planning on Investments: In the dynamic world of investments, finding strategies that resonate with your lifestyle and preferences is essential. If the intricacies of the stock market feel overwhelming or time-consuming, exploring alternative avenues like mutual funds can be a prudent choice. As a testament to this, my diversified portfolio in mutual funds has yielded consistent returns ranging between 35-39%. This illustrates that substantial financial growth can be achieved without necessarily immersing oneself in the complexities of daily market fluctuations. The key lies in adopting an investment approach that aligns with your goals and risk tolerance. Mutual funds are a popular investment option among Indian investors, as they offer several advantages, such as professional management, diversification, liquidity, and cost averaging12. According to a report by the Association of Mutual Funds in India (AMFI), the assets under management (AUM) of the mutual fund industry in India reached ₹36.59 lakh crore in October 2021, registering a growth of 41.5% year-on-year3. The report also showed that the number of systematic investment plan (SIP) accounts increased by 35.4% year-on-year to 4.32 crore, with a monthly inflow of ₹9,745 crore3. These figures indicate the growing popularity and acceptance of mutual funds as a viable investment option in India.

Strategic Real Estate Investments: Strategic planning extends beyond financial instruments to encompass tangible assets like real estate. Consider adopting an approach where your investments work synergistically to generate additional income. Drawing inspiration from personal experience, the journey began with the outright purchase of a house using available funds. The rental income generated from this property is then strategically invested in acquiring a second flat. The combined rent from both properties is now accumulating towards the acquisition of a third, smaller property. This approach exemplifies the power of leveraging existing resources to multiply assets without injecting additional capital. Strategic real estate investments can play a pivotal role in securing financial stability and fostering long-term growth. Real estate is one of the most preferred asset classes in India, as it offers capital appreciation, rental income, tax benefits, and inflation hedge4. According to a report by Knight Frank, the residential property market in India witnessed a strong recovery in the first half of 2021, with sales volume increasing by 71% year-on-year to 1.38 lakh units across eight major cities5. The report also stated that the affordable and mid-segment housing segments accounted for 72% of the total sales volume, indicating the high demand for these segments5. Moreover, the report highlighted that the warehousing and logistics sector in India also witnessed robust growth in the first half of 2021, with leasing activity increasing by 36% year-on-year to 20.1 million square feet across eight major cities6. The report attributed this growth to the rising demand from e-commerce, third-party logistics, and manufacturing sectors6. These trends suggest that the real estate sector in India offers ample opportunities for strategic investments across various segments and geographies.

In essence, the key takeaway is to align your financial actions with a holistic plan that maximizes the potential for growth and sustainability. Much like honey bees collaborating to achieve collective success, our financial strategies can benefit from a cooperative mindset. By fostering relationships with like-minded individuals and implementing strategic investments, we not only secure our financial future but also contribute to the well-being of a broader financial community. The legacy we leave behind becomes not just a personal triumph but a testament to the collaborative spirit that sustains and enriches the financial ecosystems we inhabit.

"SAVE LIKE A HONEY BEE:

10 Steps To Financial Freedom"

Set Clear Financial Goals: Just as honey bees communicate the location and quality of nectar through the waggle dance, start by identifying your short-term and long-term financial objectives. Whether it's saving for a vacation, buying a house, or retiring comfortably, articulate your goals clearly and review them regularly. For example, you can use the SMART framework to set specific, measurable, achievable, relevant, and time-bound goals. You can also use online calculators or apps to estimate how much you need to save and invest for each goal12

Create a Budget Hive: Develop a budget that allocates your income strategically. Designate specific amounts for essentials like housing, food, transportation, and entertainment. Include a portion for savings and investments based on your goals and risk tolerance. A well-structured budget serves as the hive's blueprint for financial success. According to a survey by ETMONEY, only 33% of Indians have a monthly budget, and 47% of them struggle to stick to it. The survey also found that the top reasons for not having a budget are lack of awareness, lack of discipline, and lack of motivation3 To overcome these challenges, you can use online tools or apps that help you create and manage your budget, such as ETMONEY, Walnut, or Money View.

Monitor and Adjust: Regularly track your income and expenses, comparing them to your budget. If you find yourself overspending in certain areas, adjust accordingly. Utilize online tools or apps for effective monitoring and, like bees adapting to changing conditions, make financial adjustments as needed. According to a report by Nielsen, the average monthly household expenditure in India increased by 3.8% in 2020, mainly due to higher spending on food, health, and education. The report also stated that the average monthly savings decreased by 32% in 2020, mainly due to lower income and higher expenses. To cope with these changes, you can review your budget regularly and make necessary changes to your spending and saving habits.

Evaluate Each Financial Foray: Before making any financial decision, evaluate its impact on your goals. Ask questions like, "Do I really need this?" and "How will this affect my budget and long-term objectives?" Be mindful of your spending choices, mirroring the discerning nature of bees when selecting flowers. According to a report by Deloitte, the consumer behavior in India has changed significantly due to the COVID-19 pandemic, with more emphasis on health, safety, and value. The report also suggested that consumers are more likely to spend on essential items, such as groceries, medicines, and utilities, and less likely to spend on discretionary items, such as travel, dining out, and entertainment. To align your spending with your goals, you can use the 50/30/20 rule, which suggests allocating 50% of your income to needs, 30% to wants, and 20% to savings and investments.

Avoid Impulse Buying: Guard against impulsive financial decisions by implementing strategies such as waiting 24 hours before making a purchase, creating and sticking to a shopping list, and avoiding shopping when emotional or hungry. This aligns with the disciplined foraging habits of bees. According to a study by CashKaro, 71% of Indian shoppers admit to impulse buying, and 64% of them regret it later. The study also found that the top triggers for impulse buying are discounts, social media, and peer pressure. To curb your impulse buying, you can use apps that help you track your spending, such as Spendee, Money Manager, or Monefy.

Seek Value Over Quantity: Embrace the honey bee's principle of quality over quantity. Evaluate the benefits and costs of each spending decision. Spend less on things that don't add value to your life and more on those that align with your values and goals. Cultivate a discerning approach to financial choices. According to a report by KPMG, the value-conscious consumer in India is looking for products and services that offer the best value for money, quality, and convenience. The report also stated that the value-conscious consumer is willing to pay a premium for products and services that offer personalization, innovation, and sustainability. To seek value over quantity, you can use the concept of cost per use, which measures how much value you get from an item based on how often you use it. For example, if you buy a pair of shoes for ₹5,000 and wear them 100 times, the cost per use is ₹50. If you buy another pair of shoes for ₹2,000 and wear them 10 times, the cost per use is ₹200. In this case, the first pair of shoes offers more value than the second pair, even though it is more expensive.

Invest in Experiences: Similar to bees investing time and effort in creating honey, allocate resources to experiences that bring joy and enrichment. Research shows that spending on experiences, such as travel or education, contributes more significantly to long-term happiness than material possessions. According to a study by Booking.com, 65% of Indian travelers plan to travel more in the future to make up for the lost time due to the pandemic, and 47% of them prefer to spend their money on experiences rather than material items. The study also found that 70% of Indian travelers want to travel more sustainably in the future, and 68% of them want to have more authentic and local experiences. To invest in experiences, you can use platforms that offer curated and personalized travel packages, such as MakeMyTrip, Yatra, or Cleartrip. You can also use platforms that offer online courses and certifications, such as Coursera, Udemy, or edX.

Save and Invest Wisely: Develop the habit of saving and investing systematically. Build emergency funds, contribute to retirement plans, and diversify your investments. Like bees storing honey for the winter, create financial reserves that can sustain you during unforeseen challenges. According to a report by SBI, the household savings rate in India increased to 21% in 2020, compared to 18.2% in 2019, mainly due to lower consumption and higher precautionary savings. The report also stated that the household financial liabilities decreased to 3.4% in 2020, compared to 4% in 2019, mainly due to lower borrowing and higher repayment. To save and invest wisely, you can use platforms that offer various financial products and services, such as Zerodha, Groww, or Paytm Money. You can also use platforms that offer financial planning and advisory services, such as Scripbox, Kuvera, or ETMONEY.

Continuous Financial Education: Be committed to ongoing financial education. Understand different investment avenues, stay informed about market trends, and seek professional advice when needed. A knowledgeable approach to finance mirrors the informed dances of bees that communicate critical information. According to a report by Standard & Poor's, only 24% of adults in India are financially literate, which is lower than the global average of 33%. The report also stated that the financial literacy rate in India varies significantly by gender, education, income, and location. To improve your financial education, you can use platforms that offer financial news, analysis, and insights, such as Moneycontrol, Economic Times, or Livemint. You can also use platforms that offer financial podcasts, videos, or blogs, such as Paisa Vaisa, The Money Show, or Jago Investor.

Practice Gratitude for Financial Well-being: Cultivate gratitude for your financial journey. Acknowledge the effort that goes into earning and managing money. Express thanks for your income, expenses, and savings. Gratitude enhances your financial well-being and aligns with the mindful nature of honey bees within their hive. According to a study by Berkeley, gratitude can improve financial decision-making, increase generosity, and reduce materialism. The study also suggested that gratitude can reduce stress, increase happiness, and improve physical and mental health. To practice gratitude, you can use apps that help you record and reflect on the things you are grateful for, such as Gratitude, Presently, or Bliss. You can also use apps that help you donate or share your wealth with others, such as GiveIndia, Milaap, or Ketto.

Adopting these "Save Like a Honey Bee" principles can pave the way for financial freedom, empowering you to navigate economic seasons with resilience and leave a legacy that echoes the collaborative and sustainable spirit of a hive.

Disclaimer: The information provided in this chapter is for general guidance and educational purposes only. It is not intended to be a substitute for professional financial advice, planning, or management

EPILOGUE:

FORGING YOUR FINANCIAL FLIGHT PATH

Throughout this book, we have explored the fascinating world of honey bees and how they can inspire us to achieve financial abundance. We have learned from their wisdom, resilience, and collaboration, and applied their principles to our own financial endeavors. We have seen how strategic planning, mindful spending, and nurturing a legacy can help us craft a trajectory towards financial freedom.

As we conclude this book, it's time to look ahead and chart our own financial flight path. "Save Like a Honey Bee: Harnessing Nature's Wisdom for Financial Abundance" has been our guiding light, but it is not the final destination. Each of us has a unique financial journey, shaped by our goals, circumstances, and preferences. Therefore, we need to seek professional advice that is tailored to our specific needs and situations.

Financial advisors, like seasoned beekeepers, have the expertise and experience to guide us through the complexities and uncertainties of the financial hive. They can help us navigate the diverse and dynamic financial landscapes, like the blossoms in a meadow, and find the best opportunities and solutions for us. They can also help us avoid the pitfalls and risks that may arise along the way, and protect our financial assets and legacy.

A Gentle Reminder and a Disclaimer:

This book is intended to provide a roadmap, not a substitute, for personalized financial advice. The author has drawn from the collective wisdom of bees and various sources to share insights and tips that can inspire and inform our financial decision-making. However, the author does not claim to have all the answers, nor does the book cover all the aspects and scenarios of financial planning.

The financial landscapes are subject to change, and external factors may influence the outcomes of our decisions. The journey to financial well-being requires continuous learning and adaptation. We need to stay updated and aware of the changing economic conditions and trends, and adjust our strategies and actions accordingly.

Each reader's financial situation is unique, requiring a customized approach. The examples, proverbs, and data presented in the book are illustrative, not prescriptive. They are meant to demonstrate the principles and concepts discussed in the book, not to provide specific recommendations or solutions. Always consider consulting with financial professionals who can provide personalized advice based on your goals, risk tolerance, and financial circumstances.

In the spirit of the honey bee, let's embark on this financial journey with diligence, resilience, and a collaborative mindset. May our collective efforts yield sweet fruits of financial abundance, securing prosperous futures for ourselves and generations to come.

Illustrating Financial Decisions Through Examples, Proverbs, and Data:

Car Purchase: One of the major financial decisions we face is whether to buy a new car with a loan or a used car with cash. This decision involves researching the costs, benefits, and long-term impacts of each option. A new car may offer more features, comfort, and reliability, but it also comes with a higher price tag, interest payments, and depreciation. A used car may be more affordable, but it may also have more maintenance issues, lower resale value, and less warranty coverage. An abrupt decision, based on impulse or emotion, may lead to regrettable consequences, such as debt, stress, or buyer's remorse. Therefore, it is important to make an informed choice, based on our needs, budget, and preferences.

Investment Portfolio: Another major financial decision we face is how to invest our money for long-term growth. This decision requires thorough research and analysis of the various investment options available to us. One of the key factors to consider is diversification, which means spreading our money across different types of assets, such as stocks, bonds, mutual funds, etc. Diversification can help us reduce the risk and volatility of our portfolio, and increase the chances of stable returns. Investing in a single stock, on the other hand, exposes us to more risk and uncertainty, as the stock price may fluctuate significantly due to market conditions, company performance, or other factors. An abrupt decision, based on hype or speculation, may lead to disastrous results, such as losing our money, missing out on better opportunities, or facing legal troubles. Therefore, it is important to make a prudent choice, based on our risk tolerance, time horizon, and financial goals.

"A stitch in time saves nine":* This proverb aligns with the financial planning principle of taking early and timely actions to secure our financial future. By starting to save and invest as soon as possible, we can take advantage of the power of compounding, which means earning interest on our interest, and growing our money exponentially over time. By preparing for unexpected events and emergencies, we can avoid the stress and costs of dealing with them later. By planning for our retirement and legacy, we can ensure that we have enough income and assets to support our lifestyle and our loved ones. Household savings trends in India, as reported by SBI, indicate a growing awareness of the need for financial preparedness, especially in the wake of the COVID-19 pandemic. The report shows that the household savings rate increased from 18.2% in 2019-20 to 21% in 2020-21, reflecting a shift in consumer behavior towards more saving and less spending.

"Don't put all your eggs in one basket":* This proverb emphasizes the importance of diversification in financial stability. By spreading our money across different types of assets, we can reduce the risk of losing everything if one asset fails or underperforms. We can also benefit from the different returns and characteristics of each asset, and balance our portfolio according to our risk and return preferences. Trends in consumer behavior in India, highlighted by KPMG, echo the proverb, with more individuals seeking diversified consumption choices and prioritizing value over quantity. The report states that consumers are looking for more variety, quality, and convenience in their purchases, and are willing to pay more for products and services that meet their needs and expectations.

As we weave these lessons into our financial fabric, may we all enjoy the sweet rewards of prudent decisions and sustainable financial growth.

EXERCISE 1

ASSESSING YOUR INVESTMENT MINDSET

Your mindset towards investment is a key factor that influences your financial decisions. It reflects your beliefs, attitudes, and behaviors related to investing. By understanding your mindset, you can identify your strengths and weaknesses, and improve your investment outcomes. This comprehensive exercise will help you assess your investment mindset and explore ways to enhance it. You will need a pen and paper or a digital document to write down your responses.

Section 1: Reflecting on Beliefs and Attitudes

Your beliefs and attitudes are the foundation of your investment mindset. They shape how you view money, wealth, risk, and returns. They also affect how you react to market fluctuations and investment opportunities. In this section, you will reflect on your core beliefs and attitudes about investing.

1. *What are your fundamental beliefs about money and wealth?*

Some possible questions to guide your reflection are:

- What does money mean to you? Is it a tool, a goal, a reward, a burden, or something else?

- How do you define wealth? Is it a number, a lifestyle, a state of mind, or something else?

- What are the sources of your beliefs about money and wealth? Are they influenced by your family, culture, education, religion, or personal experiences?

- How do your beliefs about money and wealth affect your investment decisions? Do they motivate you, limit you, or challenge you?

Write down your responses in a few sentences.

2. *How do you perceive risk? Are you risk-averse, risk-neutral, or risk-seeking? Why?*

Some possible questions to guide your reflection are:

- How do you measure risk? Do you use quantitative methods, such as standard deviation, beta, or Sharpe ratio, or qualitative methods, such as gut feeling, intuition, or expert opinion?
- How do you manage risk? Do you diversify your portfolio, hedge your positions, set stop-loss orders, or use other strategies?
- How do you cope with risk? Do you embrace it, avoid it, or balance it?
- What are the factors that influence your risk perception? Are they related to your personality, goals, circumstances, or emotions?

Write down your responses in a few sentences.

3. *What is your attitude towards long-term versus short-term gains?*

Some possible questions to guide your reflection are:

- What is your time horizon for investing? Do you invest for the short term (less than a year), medium term (1-5 years), or long term (more than 5 years)?
- What are your expectations for returns? Do you aim for high returns, moderate returns, or low returns?
- How do you balance growth and income in your

portfolio? Do you prefer capital appreciation, dividend income, or a mix of both?

- How do you deal with volatility and uncertainty in the market? Do you stay invested, exit the market, or adjust your portfolio?

Write down your responses in a few sentences.

4. *Consider your past experiences with investments. How have they shaped your current beliefs and attitudes?*

Some possible questions to guide your reflection are:

- What are the most memorable or impactful investments you have made? How did they perform? How did they make you feel?
- What are the most valuable or useful lessons you have learned from your investments? How did they change your perspective or behavior?
- What are the most common or recurring mistakes you have made in your investments? How did they affect your results or confidence?
- What are the most challenging or difficult situations you have faced in your investments? How did you overcome them or learn from them?

Write down your responses in a few sentences.

Section 2: Identifying Financial Goals and Objectives

Your financial goals and objectives are the destination of your investment journey. They define what you want to achieve, why you want to achieve it, and how you plan to achieve it. They also help you align your investment decisions with your overall life goals. In this section, you will identify your financial goals and objectives and evaluate their suitability and feasibility.

1. *List your short-term financial goals (1-3 years), medium-term goals (3-10 years), and long-term goals (10+ years).*

Some possible examples of financial goals are:

- Saving for an emergency fund, a vacation, or a wedding
- Paying off debt, such as credit cards, student loans, or mortgages
- Buying a home, a car, or a business
- Funding education, such as college, graduate school, or professional courses
- Investing for retirement, such as 401(k), IRA, or pension
- Building wealth, such as net worth, assets, or income
- Creating a legacy, such as estate planning, charitable giving, or family support

Write down your financial goals in a table format, such as:

Time Horizon	Financial Goal	Amount Needed
Short Term	Save for a vacation	$5,000
Medium Term	Pay off student loans	$50,000
Long Term	Invest for retirement	$1,000,000

2. *For each goal, indicate the level of risk you are willing to take.*

The level of risk you are willing to take depends on your risk perception, as discussed in Section 1, as well as your time horizon, return expectations, and portfolio composition. Generally, the longer your time horizon, the higher the risk you can afford to take, as you have more time to recover from losses and benefit from compounding. The higher your return expectations, the higher the risk you need to take, as there is a trade-off between risk and return. The more diversified your portfolio, the lower the risk you face, as you reduce the impact of any single asset or market.

Write down the level of risk you are willing to take for each goal in the same table, using a scale of 1-10, where 1 is the lowest and 10 is the highest, such as:

Time Horizon	Financial Goal	Amount Needed	Risk Level
Short Term	Save for a vacation	$5,000	2
Medium Term	Pay off student loans	$50,000	5
Long Term	Invest for retirement	$1,000,000	8

3. *Reflect on whether your investment goals align with your overall life goals. If not, what adjustments would you consider?*

Your investment goals should be consistent with your overall life goals, such as your personal, professional, and social aspirations. They should also be SMART, which means Specific, Measurable, Achievable, Relevant, and Time-bound. If your investment goals are not aligned with your life goals, or if they are not SMART, you may need to reconsider or revise them.

Write down your reflection in a few sentences, such as:

- My investment goals are mostly aligned with my life goals, except for the long-term goal of investing for retirement. I think this goal is too vague and unrealistic, as I do not have a clear idea of how much I need to save, what kind of lifestyle I want to have, or when I want to retire. I would like to make this goal more specific, measurable, achievable, relevant, and time-bound, by using a retirement calculator, setting a target retirement age, and creating a retirement plan.

- My investment goals are not aligned with my life goals, as they are too focused on short-term gains and ignore the long-term implications. I think this is because I have a high-risk, high-reward attitude, and I enjoy the thrill of trading. However, I realize that this approach may jeopardize my financial security and stability in the future. I would like to balance my investment goals with more long-term and diversified objectives, such as saving for retirement, building wealth, and creating a legacy.

Section 3: Assessing Investment Knowledge and Awareness

Your investment knowledge and awareness are the tools and resources that enable you to make informed and effective financial decisions. They include your understanding of different investment vehicles, such as stocks, bonds, mutual funds, real estate, etc., as well as your access to market trends and financial news. They also include your familiarity with investment jargon, such as terms, concepts, and formulas. In this section, you will assess your investment knowledge and awareness and identify areas for improvement or learning.

1. *Rate your current level of knowledge about different investment vehicles (stocks, bonds, mutual funds, real*

estate, etc.) on a scale of 1-10.

The level of knowledge you have about different investment vehicles depends on your education, experience, and interest in investing. Generally, the more knowledge you have, the better you can evaluate and compare the pros and cons of each option, and choose the ones that suit your goals, risk, and return preferences. However, having too much knowledge can also lead to overconfidence, analysis paralysis, or information overload, which may impair your decision-making.

Write down your rating for each investment vehicle in a table format, such as:

Investment Vehicle	Knowledge Level
Stocks	7
Bonds	5
Mutual Funds	6
Real Estate	4

2. *How do you stay informed about market trends and financial news?*

Staying informed about market trends and financial news is important for keeping up with the changes and opportunities in the financial world. It can help you identify potential risks and rewards, adjust your portfolio, and make timely decisions. However, staying informed also requires filtering and interpreting the information, as not all sources are reliable, relevant, or accurate.

Write down the sources and methods you use to stay informed, such as:

I subscribe to financial newsletters, podcasts, and blogs, such as The Wall Street Journal, The Motley Fool, and Moneycontrol, to get the latest updates and insights on the global and local markets, sectors, and companies. I also use online platforms, such as Yahoo Finance, Google Finance, and Bloomberg, to access real-time data, charts, and analysis on various investment vehicles, such as stocks, bonds, mutual funds, and real estate. Additionally, I follow social media accounts, such as Twitter, Reddit, and Quora, to interact with other investors, experts, and influencers, and learn from their opinions, experiences, and recommendations.

EXERCISE 2

MAPPING YOUR PATH TO FINANCIAL GOALS

Achieving financial goals requires strategic planning and consistent efforts. This exercise is designed to help you clarify your goals, break them down into actionable steps, and create a roadmap for success. Grab a notebook or open a digital document to record your responses.

Section 1: Define Your Financial Goals

- To identify and list your financial goals, you can use the SMART criteria, which stands for Specific, Measurable, Achievable, Relevant, and Time-bound. This means that your goals should be clear, quantifiable, realistic, aligned with your values, and have a deadline.
- To quantify each goal with a specific monetary value, you can use online calculators, such as this one, to estimate how much you need to save for different goals, such as buying a house, saving for retirement, or paying off debt. You can also use this tool to adjust your goals for inflation and taxes.

Section 2: Prioritize Your Goals

- To rank your financial goals in order of priority, you can use the ABCD method, which stands for Absolute necessity, Basic necessity, Comfort, and Desire. This means that you should prioritize the goals that are essential for your survival and well-being, such as paying for food, shelter, and health care, over the goals that are nice to have, such as traveling, buying luxury items, or donating to charity.

- To assign a timeframe for each goal, you can use the rule of thumb that short-term goals are within one to three years, medium-term goals are within three to five years, and long-term goals are more than five years away. However, you can also adjust your timeframe according to your personal situation and preferences.

Section 3: Assess Your Current Financial Situation

- To list your current sources of income, you can use your pay stubs, bank statements, tax returns, or other documents that show how much money you earn from your job, side hustles, investments, or other sources. You can also use this worksheet to track your income and expenses.

- To calculate your monthly expenses and categorize them into essential and non-essential categories, you can use your receipts, bills, credit card statements, or other records that show how much money you spend on various items, such as rent, utilities, groceries, entertainment, dining out, etc. You can also use this budget template to organize your expenses and set spending limits.

- To determine your current savings and investments, you can use your bank accounts, investment accounts, retirement accounts, or other accounts that show how much money you have saved or invested for different purposes, such as emergency fund, retirement fund, or other savings goals. You can also use this net worth calculator to measure your overall financial health.

Section 4: Break Down Goals into Actionable Steps

To achieve your financial goals, you need to break them down into smaller, manageable, and actionable steps. This will help you stay focused, motivated, and accountable. For each financial goal, outline the specific steps you need to take to achieve it. Consider potential obstacles or challenges that may arise along the way, and how you might overcome them.

For example, if one of your goals is to save $5,000 for a vacation in two years, some possible steps are:

- Set up a separate savings account for your vacation fund and automate monthly transfers from your checking account.
- Cut down on non-essential expenses, such as eating out, entertainment, and subscriptions, and redirect the savings to your vacation fund.
- Look for additional income opportunities, such as a side hustle, freelancing, or selling unwanted items, and add the extra income to your vacation fund.
- Research and compare different travel options, such as destinations, flights, hotels, and activities, and look for deals and discounts.
- Track your progress and celebrate your milestones, such as reaching 25%, 50%, or 75% of your goal.

Some potential challenges and solutions are:

- Unexpected expenses or emergencies that reduce your savings capacity. Solution: Have an emergency fund in place to cover unforeseen costs and avoid dipping into your vacation fund.
- Loss of income or reduced income that affects your ability to save. Solution: Adjust your budget and spending habits accordingly, and look for alternative sources of income or financial assistance if needed.
- Change of plans or preferences that alter your vacation goal. Solution: Reevaluate your goal and revise your steps accordingly, and communicate with anyone else involved in your vacation plan.

Write down the steps and challenges for each of your financial goals in a table format, such as:

Financial Goal	Steps	Challenges and Solutions
Save $5,000 for a vacation in two years	- Set up a separate savings account and automate monthly transfers - Cut down on non-essential expenses and redirect the savings - Look for additional income opportunities and add the extra income - Research and compare different travel options and look for deals - Track progress and celebrate milestones	- Unexpected expenses or emergencies. Solution: Have an emergency fund - Loss of income or reduced income. Solution: Adjust budget and spending habits, and look for alternative sources of income or financial assistance - Change of plans or preferences. Solution: Reevaluate goal and revise steps, and communicate with anyone else involved

Section 5: Create a Monthly Budget

A monthly budget is a key tool for managing your money and reaching your financial goals. It helps you allocate your income to different categories, such as savings, investments, debt payments, and living expenses. It also helps you monitor your spending habits and identify areas where you can save more or spend less.

To create a monthly budget, you need to:

- Develop a detailed list of your income and expenses, based on your current financial situation and your financial goals. You can use the information from Section 3 to help you with this step.

- Allocate funds to different categories, such as savings, investments, debt payments, and living expenses, based on your priorities and needs. You can use the 50/30/20 rule as a guideline, which suggests spending 50% of your income on needs, 30% on wants, and 20% on savings and investments.

- Review your budget regularly and make adjustments as needed. Compare your actual income and expenses with your budgeted amounts, and identify any gaps or discrepancies. Are there areas where you can cut expenses to allocate more towards your goals? Are there areas where you need to increase your income or adjust your goals?

You can use this budget template to create and track your monthly budget, or use a budgeting app or software of your choice.

Section 6: Explore Additional Income Streams

One way to accelerate the achievement of your financial goals is to increase your income. This can be done by exploring potential opportunities for additional income, such as a side hustle, freelancing, or investment opportunities. These can help you boost your savings, pay off your debt faster, or grow your wealth.

To explore additional income streams, you need to:

- Identify your skills, talents, interests, and passions that you can leverage to earn extra money. For example, if you are good at writing, you can offer freelance writing services, start a blog, or write an ebook. If you are passionate about photography, you can sell your photos online, teach photography classes, or start a photography business.

- Research the market demand, competition, and profitability of your potential income streams. For example, if you want to start a blog, you need to find out what topics are popular, who are your target audience, and how you can monetize your blog. If you want to sell your photos online, you need to find out what platforms are available, what are the fees and commissions, and how you can market your photos.

- Calculate how much additional income you can earn from your chosen income streams, and how this can contribute to your financial goals. For example, if you want to offer freelance writing services, you need to estimate how many hours you can work, how much you can charge, and how much you can save or invest from your earnings. If you want to sell your photos online, you need to estimate how many photos you can sell, how much you can earn, and how much you can save or invest from your earnings.

Write down your potential income streams, market research, and income calculations in a table format, such as:

Potential Income Stream	Market Research	Income Calculation
Freelance writing services	- High demand for content writing, copywriting, and editing in various niches - Competitive market with many platforms and freelancers - Profitable if you can offer quality work, build a portfolio, and attract clients	- Can work 10 hours per week on average - Can charge $25 per hour on average - Can earn $1,000 per month on average - Can save or invest $500 per month on average

Sell photos online	- High demand for stock photos, especially in categories such as travel, lifestyle, and business - Competitive market with many platforms and photographers - Profitable if you can offer unique and high-quality photos, use keywords and tags, and promote your photos	- Can upload 100 photos per month on average - Can earn $0.25 per download on average - Can earn $250 per month on average - Can save or invest $125 per month on average

Section 7: Monitor and Adjust

Creating a financial plan is not a one-time event, but a continuous process. You need to monitor your progress and adjust your plan as your circumstances change. This will help you stay on track, overcome challenges, and seize opportunities.

To monitor and adjust your financial plan, you need to:

- Establish a system for tracking your progress towards each financial goal. This could involve setting up milestones and regularly checking in on your achievements. For example, if your goal is to save $5,000 for a vacation in two years, you can set quarterly milestones of $625 and review your savings account balance every three months.

- Be prepared to adjust your strategy if circumstances change. Flexibility is key in navigating the dynamic nature of financial planning. For example, if you lose your job, you may need to reduce your expenses, tap into your emergency fund, or look for a new source of income. If you receive a windfall, you may want to increase your savings, pay off your debt, or invest more.

- Review your financial plan at least once a year, or more frequently if needed. Evaluate your current financial situation, goals, and strategies, and make any necessary changes. For example, if you achieve one of your goals, you can celebrate your success and set a new goal. If you face a new challenge, you can seek help and find a solution.

Write down your system for tracking your progress, your contingency plans for changing circumstances, and your schedule for reviewing your plan, such as:

Financial Goal	Steps	Challenges and Solutions
Save $5,000 for a vacation in two years	- Set up a separate savings account and automate monthly transfers - Cut down on non-essential expenses and redirect the savings - Look for additional income opportunities and add the extra income - Research and compare different travel options and look for deals - Track progress and celebrate milestones	- Unexpected expenses or emergencies. Solution: Have an emergency fund - Loss of income or reduced income. Solution: Adjust budget and spending habits, and look for alternative sources of income or financial assistance - Change of plans or preferences. Solution: Reevaluate goal and revise steps, and communicate with anyone else involved
Pay off $50,000 student loans in five years	- Consolidate and refinance your loans to get a lower interest rate and a single monthly payment - Increase your monthly payment by adding extra	- Rising interest rates or fees. Solution: Lock in a fixed rate and avoid late payments or penalties - Reduced income or

	income or reducing expenses - Apply any windfalls, such as bonuses, tax refunds, or gifts, to your loan balance - Use the debt avalanche method to pay off the highest-interest loan first, then move to the next one - Track your progress and celebrate your milestones, such as paying off 25%, 50%, or 75% of your debt	increased expenses. Solution: Apply for income-driven repayment plans or hardship deferment or forbearance - Temptation to spend or save instead of paying off debt. Solution: Remind yourself of your goal and the benefits of being debt-free
Invest $1,000,000 for retirement in 30 years	- Determine your retirement income needs based on your desired lifestyle and life expectancy - Contribute to tax-advantaged retirement accounts, such as 401(k), IRA, or Roth IRA, up to the annual limits - Invest in a diversified portfolio of stocks, bonds, mutual funds, and other assets, based on your risk tolerance and time horizon - Rebalance your portfolio periodically to maintain your target asset allocation and risk level - Review your retirement plan regularly and adjust your contributions, investments, and withdrawal strategies as needed	- Market volatility or downturns. Solution: Stay invested, diversify your portfolio, and avoid emotional decisions - Inflation or taxes. Solution: Invest in inflation-protected securities, such as TIPS or I-bonds, and use tax-efficient strategies, such as Roth conversions or tax-loss harvesting - Unexpected events or emergencies. Solution: Have an emergency fund, insurance, and estate plan

Conclusion: Commitment and Celebration

The final step of creating a financial plan is to reaffirm your commitment to your financial goals and plan for small celebrations as you achieve milestones along the way. This will help you stay motivated, focused, and positive throughout your financial journey.

To reaffirm your commitment to your financial goals, you need to:

- Reflect on the importance and benefits of each goal and how it will improve your life and well-being. For example, if your goal is to pay off your student loans, you can think about how it will free up your cash flow, reduce your stress, and increase your credit score.

- Write down your goals and display them in a visible place, such as your fridge, desk, or phone. This will remind you of your goals and keep you accountable.

- Share your goals with someone you trust, such as a family member, friend, or financial planner. This will provide you with support, feedback, and encouragement.

To plan for small celebrations as you achieve milestones, you need to:

- Define what constitutes a milestone for each goal, such as reaching a certain percentage, amount, or date. For example, if your goal is to invest $1,000,000 for retirement in 30 years, you can set milestones of $100,000, $250,000, $500,000, and $750,000.

- Decide how you will reward yourself for each milestone, such as treating yourself to a meal, a movie, or a gift. The reward should be something that you enjoy and value, but not something that will derail your progress or budget.

- Celebrate your achievements and acknowledge your efforts, such as by expressing gratitude, sharing your success, or updating your plan.

Remember, creating a financial plan is not a one-time event, but a continuous process. You need to monitor your progress and adjust your plan as your circumstances change. This will help you stay on track, overcome challenges, and seize opportunities. By following the steps outlined in this exercise, you can create a comprehensive and personalized financial plan that will help you achieve your financial goals and dreams.

Write to shamsud.ahmed@gmail.com

ABOUT THE AUTHOR

Shamsud Zaman

Shamsud Zaman Ahmed, a literary journeyman, initiated his odyssey with words at the age of 8 under the unwavering encouragement of his mother. What began as a childhood passion has evolved into a distinguished writing career, seamlessly interwoven with over 20 years of corporate experience. Shamsud is not merely an accomplished author, but a strategic  professional deeply involved in numerous process improvement projects, sculpting new models and structures for organizational excellence.

An MBA holder from Brussels, Shamsud's literary prowess extends beyond traditional boundaries. He stands as a significant contributor to numerous poetry collections, showcasing his versatility in the realm of verse. His impact reverberates in the digital landscape, evident in several impactful eBooks that highlight his adaptability in the contemporary literary scene.

Occupying a demanding position within a global telecom giant has not deterred Shamsud's commitment to his craft. His written achievements include not only poetry but also screenwriting, with over 15 episodes contributed to the TV series "Jibon. com" for a local channel in Assam.

Beyond literature, Shamsud finds solace in the company of his two children, Arianna and Zayden. Supported by his wife, he views family as an invaluable pillar of support and motivation. This duality in dedication underscores a man adept at navigating the realms of creativity and responsibility.

Engrossed in crafting his untitled Crime Thriller scheduled for release in 2024, Shamsud also channels his creativity into the world of painting whenever time permits. Moreover, he is fervently working on his groundbreaking book, "BARE MAXIMUM," introducing a concept set to inspire those seeking to break free from mediocrity and embrace the extraordinary.

BOOKS BY THIS AUTHOR

'Bare Maximum': A Survival Tactic In The Modern World Where Less Can Be More!

Embark on a profound journey of personal and professional transformation with "BARE MAXIMUM" by Shamsud Zaman Ahmed. This groundbreaking book challenges conventional thinking and introduces readers to the revolutionary concept of Maximilism. Here's what you can expect:

1. **Mindset Revolution:** Dive into the exploration of Maximilism, a mindset that transcends mediocrity and propels individuals toward unparalleled excellence. Discover how a shift in mindset can lead to transformative outcomes.

2. **Corporate Wisdom:** Gain unique insights into infusing Maximilism into the corporate world. Explore strategies for fostering creativity, reshaping strategic thinking, and driving innovation within organizational structures.

3. **Personal Growth Narratives:** Navigate through personal growth stories that demonstrate the power of adopting a Maximilist approach. Learn how challenges can become stepping stones for success and how resilience can lead to extraordinary achievements.

4. **Balancing Act:** Uncover the secrets of balancing family and professional life while maintaining a Maximilist ethos. Explore how individuals can find joy and fulfillment in multifaceted

commitments without compromising on excellence.

What to Expect:
- **Inspirational Narratives:** Engaging and inspiring stories that resonate with readers from all walks of life.
- **Actionable Strategies:** Practical wisdom and actionable strategies to implement Maximilism in both personal and professional spheres.
- **Innovative Thinking:** A call to challenge conventional norms, fostering innovative thinking and unlocking untapped potential.

Are you ready to embrace Maximilism? "BARE MAXIMUM" is not just a book; it's a revolution in mindset and a guide to unlocking the extraordinary within. The journey begins now.

Synergetic Mastery : The Fusion Path To Holistic Growth

Embark on a transformative journey with "Synergetic Mastery." This book introduces a framework integrating Emotional Alchemy, Purposeful Creativity, and Legacy Engineering for unprecedented success in every facet of life. Real-world examples, success metrics, and the inspiring story of Alex showcase the tangible benefits. The concluding chapter encourages embracing an interconnected approach for holistic and sustainable success.

Interactive Elements:

- **Innovative Games:**
Engage in complex games designed for individuals and corporate settings, making the learning experience immersive and enjoyable.

- **Series Integration:**
Seamlessly fitting into Shamsud Zaman Ahmed's series "BARE

MAXIMUM," the book introduces concepts that bridge the realms of creativity and responsibility.

Author's Bio:
Shamsud Zaman Ahmed, an MBA holder and accomplished author with over two decades of corporate experience, weaves words that transcend boundaries. His commitment is evident in his upcoming Crime Thriller and the groundbreaking series "BARE MAXIMUM."

Conclusion:
"Synergetic Mastery" is a transformative experience empowering you to navigate life with resilience, creativity, and purpose. Uncover the blueprint for holistic success in this synergistic journey towards unprecedented growth.

Ascendance: Celebrities On The Global Stage: "From Shadows To Spotlights: Stories Of Global Stardom, One Journey At A Time

"Ascendance: Celebrities on the Global Stage" is an illuminating book series that intricately weaves together the captivating narratives of individuals who have ascended to the pinnacle of global stardom. With each volume dedicated to a diverse set of luminaries, readers embark on a journey through the varied landscapes of the entertainment, sports, and cultural spheres. From the electrifying rise of South Korean phenomenon BTS to the dynamic journey of Priyanka Chopra bridging the East and West, and the magnetic allure of Dwayne "The Rock" Johnson commanding the Hollywood spotlight, the series paints a vivid tapestry of triumph against the odds.

Through meticulous research and firsthand accounts, "Ascendance" unveils the personal struggles, transformative moments, and defining choices that propelled these celebrities onto the international stage. The pages come alive with stories of perseverance, resilience, and the universal themes that resonate with audiences worldwide. Delving beyond the glitz and glamour, the series explores the impact these individuals have made, not only in their respective industries but on the cultural fabric of nations across the globe.

As readers turn each page, they encounter the authentic voices of these global icons, presented through memorable quotes, exclusive interviews, and behind-the-scenes anecdotes. "Ascendance" is not merely a chronicle of fame but a celebration of the indomitable spirit that propels individuals to transcend boundaries, inspiring others to dream bigger and reach for the stars.

With its rich storytelling and insightful exploration of the human experience behind the celebrity facade, "Ascendance: Celebrities on the Global Stage" invites readers to witness the ascent of extraordinary individuals who have left an indelible mark on the world. It's a tapestry of dreams, struggles, and triumphs, offering a front-row seat to the ascendance of those who dared to reach for greatness on the grandest stage of all.

Printed in Great Britain
by Amazon

43331571R00069